DREAM IT FIRST:
THE 80/20 LAW
TO MANIFESTATION OF
DREAMS AND GOALS

by JACQUELINE R. ROBERTSON,
"The Dream Sister"

A Phenomenal Key to Personal Change

Strategic Book Publishing and Rights Co.

Strategic Book Publishing and Rights Co.
12620 FM 1960, Suite A4-507
Houston TX 77065

www.sbpra.com

ISBN: 978-1-60976-392-3

Design: Dedicated Book Services, Inc. (www.netdbs.com)

DEDICATION

To my son, Raymond Degaston Jones II

TABLE OF CONTENTS

ACKNOWLEDGEMENTS

During the preceding six years of my life I have experienced what many would label a never-ending saga of unprecedented events.

This was a chronic, twisting, six-year divorce battle to dissolve a marriage that was much shorter than the time it took to end, where I was "losing," it appeared, everything tangible that I had accomplished in the preceding seven years of my life. "It was the best of times, it was the worst of times" all at the same time, to borrow a classic line from the book *A Tale of Two Cities* by Charles Dickens. Yet, over this dark yet mystic, time, I've been given the beautiful enlightenment of this book, a book that's truly applicable to all aspects of anyone's life, dreams, and goals I proudly present to all of my readers. I have, during the past eight years of my life, without my own awareness, been subconsciously writing this book. Yet not until the last four years have I consciously begun to formulate all the information I present. My deep-hearted acknowledgement and gratitude goes to the following people who, even without their full awareness, have aided me—directly, as well as indirectly—in writing and completing this book. I give these special acknowledgements:

To Adriana Corpus, my past secretary and friend for the last ten years, who, without her friendship, love, support, and her adept computer skills, I would not have been able to write and complete this book. I thank you.

To Patrick Earthly, my business partner and friend, whose non-judgmental listening ear, love, understanding, and support during the first year and half of our association, reignited me with that lost capacity to feel, dream, and embrace life again. I thank you.

To Patricia Nelson, my "Naomi," a friend, and next-door neighbor for the past 20 years, whose support, watchful monitoring, unwavering love, and mentorship have always been there for me. I thank you.

To the proven confidants in my family, my brother, Toney R. Brooks, and my two cousins Rodney and Hoover Jakes, whose upbeat positive minds and moral support have always been just a quick cell call away. I thank you.

To the members of The Spiritual Enrichment Center, whose congregation and library—although small—has given me much in life. I thank you.

I write this book in loving memory of my long gone, but never forgotten, parents, Carliss and Molly Robertson, And also in memory of my late husband Raymond D. Jones, Sadie Brooks, Fannie Mae Green, Reginald Ambrose, and William and Sam Brooks.

I give thanks to the following individuals in my family: my son Raymond and grandchildren Rayanne, Toshiayna, and RayJan Jones; my siblings Toney, Lily, Linda, and Sadie; my family, the Jakes, the Hudsons, the Brookses, the Robertsons, the Ambroses, the Jones's, the Hiblers, the Collinses, the Rodents, the Corleys, the Stanleys, the Stevensons, and the Chapman-Paynes.

I give further thanks to my family of friends: the Gomez family, the Corpus family, the Nelson family, the Earthly family, the Russell-Drumgole family, the Kruppa family, the Shimshon-David family. Also, to all my past and present real estate, paralegal clients, and patients that I have treated in the field of occupational therapy during my twenty-two year career. I give further thanks to all my present and past business associates, employees, friends, and neighbors that I have encountered in life; without my naming you here, you know who you are. I thank you.

Professional gratitude goes to Susan Levin and Jack Barnard of Speaker Services, Patsy Bellah of Bellah Book Support Services, book consultant Jean-Noel Bassior, Redlands Toastmaster Club 105, and my editor and publisher, AEG Publishing Group.

Lastly, although always first in my life, I give thanks to God for his inspiration and guidance in my writing and completing of this beautiful book.

Foreword

"THIS LAW SHALL OPEN UNTO THEE GOOD TREA-
SURE, THE HEAVEN TO GIVE RAIN UNTO THY LAND
IN ITS SEASON, AND TO BLESS ALL THE WORK OF
YOUR HAND; AND YOU SHALL LEND UNTO MANY
NATIONS, AND YOU SHALL NOT BORROW"

FOR IT IS:

"THE LAW'S BLESSINGS TO MAKE YOU RICH AND
TO ADD NO SORROW WITH IT"

SO:

"WHAT SO EVER YOU PRAY AND ASK BELIEVE
THAT YOU HAVE RECEIVED THEM AND YOU SHALL
HAVE THEM."

"ONCE YOU HAVE ID YOUR KEY 20 PERCENTS

IN YOUR LIFE"

So, Dreamers, let's get started!

CHAPTER 1: INTRODUCTION

As I speak to numerous business, as well as non-business, audiences often as their key motivational speaker, many have called me the "Dream Sister" and some will only refer to me as the "Dream Manifestation Expert." WHY?
BECAUSE
I know that the entire secret to every aspect of anyone's life, I mean every single aspect of anyone's life, has to do with a little effort we have accessible to us called "dreaming," and that we often refer to as our "dreams" and "goals" in life. I know, in fact, that if one hasn't built a bigger or even better dream or goal in their lives, bigger or better than any nightmares that they may be currently experiencing, or have experienced over time in their lives, then those unwanted dreams are surely the "nightmares" they're going to have carry in life. I have had numerous personal successes and dreams manifest themselves over time during my fifty-plus years. Those wonderful enlightened dreams of being a wife, a mother, a grandmother, a mortgage-free homeowner, an international traveler, a "student of spirituality," and the benefactor of many finer personal dreams and amenities have all come true in my lifetime, as well as having numerous career and business triumphs. Many of those triumphs include being a Professional Business/Motivational Speaker, published author, a Certified/Licensed Occupational Therapy Practitioner (COTA), a Licensed Real Estate Agent and Broker, a real estate investor, a Licensed Insurance Agent, a Certified/Bonded Paralegal, a Notary Public, a Licensed Residential Care Administrator, as well as concurrently owning and operating two licensed care facilities for the developmentally disabled, along with owning businesses in the women health and fitness, real estate, and the legal profession. Still, over time, I have overcome many challenges en route to all those enlightened dreams and goals, namely

what could have been a life-altering event of being medically diagnosed (as a child) and labeled as having a hearing and speech impairment, which gravely affected my expressive oral communication skills. I also endured the sudden loss of both my parents at the age of seventeen, the sudden loss of my spouse of twenty-one years of marriage to cancer, and shortly thereafter, my only son receiving a near-fatal gunshot wound to the head. And, most recently, I painstakingly endured what appeared at that time to be a never-ending, twisting, and gruesome six-year divorce saga where I let go (some would say "lost") an over 1.5-million-dollar estate that I had worked to build in the preceding seven years of my life. Still, none of these tragic nightmares and unfortunate events that have occurred over the time in my life has ever been able to prevent or slightly deter me from obtaining and reaching even more personal and professional growth and successes in my life, and thereafter effortlessly turbo-bursting any of my enlightened dreams into existence. Many people have asked me time and time again this twanging, however, merited question: "Jacqueline, just how have you, seemingly without much effort at all, been able to manage so many, nightmares in such small intervals of time over your life, yet still stay focused on turbo-bursting so many concurrent dreams?" Well, this book you're now commencing to read will surely answer this complex, yet much merited question!

Yes, every true dream and goal you hold for your life, regardless of any apparent present or past nightmare in your life, can indeed become yours. Those dreams can easily and quickly now become yours for your simple taking and acceptance when you know how to identify and use those mysterious and key hidden things invisibly nested, often without your awareness, in every area of your daily life, mysteriously with little of your own efforts giving you your greater results over shorter intervals of time in your life. I will show you how.

Truly, every one of us is indeed dreaming, as I have done in life, but many over the time in their lives have, indeed, fallen by the wayside in quickly accelerating the manifestation of their enlightened dreams while they sit in their nightmares, idly watching others appear to have, only in small intervals of time over their lives, dream after dream manifest, all with what appears to be a only a 20 percent, or less, effort.

One has to wonder at times, is there some big secret, a candle destiny, to this thing called "dreaming and success," only available to 20 percent of the population, while the other 80 percent in the world continues to wallow in their nightmares, spending years, exerting and forcing one hundred percent of their efforts, including time, money, energy, focus, and other resources, only to achieve little of the personal, health, financial, career or family goals and dreams they truly want and desire in life? Well, the answer to this also twanging, yet much merited, "Absolutely no, when any reader of this little book finds how to quickly isolate, identify, and then use for themselves those mysterious and hidden key things invisibly nested, and readily available, in every single area of their lives that are mysteriously, often without their awareness, providing them their greater results with less of their own physical efforts over smaller intervals of time now in their lives. You will now see this unfold to you in this book. Your dreams in any and all areas of your present life will, in a very short time period, despite any of your present or past circumstances, effortlessly begin to quickly multiply all your desires of health, prosperity, and abundance in all areas of your life, with you using only a mere 20 percent more of your own efforts.

The mere dream and goal of my writing this book has come about as an indirect result of my having numerous successes in life (as well as failures), over short, as well as, long intervals of time over my life. Which all actually started simply with a mere ideal (this 20 percent effort) one which has now effortlessly manifested into this beautiful book, all by my simply applying and leveraging (over time) all the spiritual laws that are now being unfolded to you here. Initially, though, it appeared as if I lacked the "intangible" means, that is, the mental "know-how," the available time, and even the initial mind-set, because of the twanging and apparent "nightmares" in my life. Yet over time by my implementing and allowing, the key spiritual laws now being presented here in this little book to go to work on my behalf, I have been able to effortlessly manifest another beautiful dream, this book you're now preparing to read.

I have no reservations at all that you, or anyone else who's looking for their true dreams and goals to quickly and effortlessly now in their lives become a tangible manifestation, will, by way of the "Law of Attraction," be attracted to this book, a little key (20 percent) more effort for anyone to use to guide them effortlessly to their long-awaited dreams and goals in their lives, which, in a very short time frame become a real tangible manifestation. It gives me great pleasure to present and share with you here:

"DREAM IT FIRST"

"THE 80/20 Law to Manifestation of your dreams and goals in your life," written by me, especially for you . . .

SO, DREAMERS, LET'S GET STARTED!

CHAPTER 2: AN INTRODUCTION TO THE 80/20 LAW

To begin this book, I would like to introduce to you a very mysterious law, an invisible law with which you may not be familiar, which has mysteriously, even without your awareness, been invisibly working on your behalf in your life. It has quickly over time brought your dreams in life closer to you, or has over time pushed those same dreams away. When this law is properly isolated, identified, and used, it will begin to quickly and effortlessly go to work for you to achieve every single dream you have or will ever desire in life. This will happen regardless of any apparent present negative circumstances or past events in your life. I will show you how in this chapter. This mysterious law, which is universally accessible to each of us, has often been referred to as "Pereto's Principle," named after the 19ᵗʰ century sociologist/economist who first discovered this law. It is more commonly heard of as the economic "80/20 Rule" that many apply in business. Whether referred to as a "principle" or "rule" by many, I will only refer to this mysterious law, in this book, as a "spiritual law": "The 80/20 Spiritual Law." As all "laws," whether they're spiritual, physical, or natural laws, are in fact invisible neutral laws that over time will provide either positive or negative effects, depending on how they are used. These scientific laws have, in fact, been proven to be absolute when their mythology, and the philosophies behind their mythology, is applied. These and other scientific laws over time have provided us in society with phenomenal rapid change and accelerated growth, as you will now see happen in your own life simply by you now using this fertile 80/20 Law.

How this mysterious spiritual law works and the simple philosophy of (and behind) this mysterious "80/20 Law" is that:

"Approximately 80 percent of all your results in life over time will flow from only approximately 20 percent of your efforts."

What is this 80/20 Law really saying?

YOU GET MORE OVER TIME WITH LESS.

WHY?

BECAUSE

APPROXIMATELY 80 PERCENT EFFORT IN ANY-THING OVER TIME GIVES OR ALLOWS YOU AP-PROXIMATELY ONLY 20 PERCENT RESULTS IN ANYTHING YOU'RE SEEKING TO ACHIEVE IN LIFE.

OR THAT

APPROXIMATELY ONLY 20 PERCENT EFFORT IN ANYTHING OVER TIME GIVES OR ALLOWS YOU AP-PROXIMATELY 80 PERCENT RESULTS IN ANYTHING YOU'RE SEEKING TO ACHIEVE IN LIFE.

Although the above statements may not adhere to your logical way of thinking, the following statements below, which further defines and paraphrases what this "80/20 Law" really means and is actually saying, may, as well, not adhere to your same reasoning or thinking.

WHAT THIS "80/20 LAW" MEANS, AND IS FACTU-ALLY SAYING. IS THAT:

1. Little (over time) = much
2. Much (over time) = little
3. Less than (over time) = greater than
4. Greater than (over time) = less than
5. One hundred percent effort (in anything over time) = less
6. One hundred percent perfection (in anything over time) = less

Why are all the above statements true?

SIMPLY BECAUSE

YOU WILL ALWAYS GET MORE "OVER TIME" WITH LESS

OR

YOU WILL ALWAYS GET LESS "OVER TIME" WITH MORE

IN ALL AREAS OF LIFE.

SIMPLY BECAUSE

APPROXIMATELY 80 PERCENT OF ALL YOUR RE-SULTS IN LIFE OVER TIME, WILL FLOW OR COME FROM APPROXIMATELY ONLY 20 PERCENT OF YOUR EFFORTS

OR

APPROXIMATELY ONLY 20 PERCENT OF ALL YOUR RESULTS IN LIFE OVER TIME WILL FLOW OR COME FROM APPROXIMATELY 80 PERCENT OF YOUR EFFORTS.

Yes, believe it or not, it is factually sound that we actually over time do receive or achieve approximately only 20 percent, or less, results of what we want, or do not want, over the time in our lives, with approximately 80 percent, or more of our efforts, in a shorter or either longer interval of time over our lives. This same statement reversed says, with approximately 80 percent, or more, effort, in an either shorter or longer interval of time (over or in) the time of our lives we receive or achieve, approximately only 20 percent, or less, results in what we want, or do not want in life, depending all on the conditions in which we use this invisible and neutral law in our lives. This law, as indicated in number five above, implies that one hundred percent effort (called Force) in anything is virtually useless (over time) in providing only (approximately) 20 percent, or even less of what you do want, in, any area of life, and (approximately) 80 percent, or even more of what you do not want in life.

As shown in number six above, seeking perfection (one hundred percent results) in anything in life over time, in fact, gives us more diminishing returns of the one hundred percent we may want, or may be seeking to achieve. This is the true reason behind the old cliché that "nothing in life is perfect." So if something or even someone in your life has appeared over time to be "picture perfect," always look for the lesser diminishing returns it, or they, may give over time, as well. This point easily brings to my mind the beautiful movie written and produced by Tyler Perry called *Why Did I Get Married*, where this 80/20 law in action could be prevalently seen or recognized. "The guy in the movie leaves his estranged wife for what appeared to be a one hundred percent perfect asset in a new woman, as this woman was a flawless "Brick House" beauty. This later "over time" resulted in the husband getting even less than 20 percent of what he really needed and wanted in a mate. He reluctantly found out, much too late, over time that his estranged wife, whom he left for this other woman, did in fact possess approximately 80 percent or more of what he always needed and wanted in a woman, but had not yet identified. Yet another man over time identified this 80 percent asset, "a diamond in the rough," and later married his newly found 80 percent asset, and "lived happily ever after," leaving the estranged ex-husband with the little "20 percent" he had found.

In any of the above presented cases, by using this fertile and mysterious "80/20 Law," those results you, or anyone else, over any long or short gap of time now (in your life) will be approximately 20 percent or 80 percent positive results of what you want or are seeking to achieve, or approximately 80 percent or 20 percent negative results of what you're not seeking or do not want in your life. Again, this is all depending on how one uses this mysterious fertile and neutral 80/20 Law in their lives. Even the physical law of "gravity" is, in fact, a neutral and invisible law, meaning it will work for you, or against you. In the case of "gravity," a law that we all learned about in grade school, it will give the positive effect, or results of holding a small glass over time in place on your kitchen counter without any of your physical effort at all, for your benefit, with its invisible powerful force, or it can have the opposite (negative) effect, resulting in quickly (without time) pulling that same glass container down towards the center of the earth (to your floor), to deter your benefit, with its same invisible and powerful force, if physical effort is applied by you simply changing the condition or position of that glass container. All this, of course, will happen depending on how one (over time) uses this law for or against him!

All the uncanny statistics and information presented above simply again reveals that we indeed will always over time get more in life with less. There is really no need to "force" one hundred percent results or perfection in any person, place, or thing in life. If one does find him or herself over time in his life forcing or seeking one hundred percent perfection in any situation in life (or exerting this one hundred percent effort), they must now know that this is really called "force," which has most likely over time, even without their awareness, provided them little positive results in what they are seeking to achieve, and possibly even more negative results in what they're seeking to achieve overall in life. This is the reason for the old cliché that "Force is always negative." Isn't this "80/20 law" an awesome and beautiful discovery?

So with this (possible new) defining discovery know that if you're now looking for your true dream(s) to be enlightened, or if you're simply seeking to more quickly accelerate, as well as effortlessly build more faith and belief in a dream or goal that's already been enlightened to you, then there's really only a little (an approximately 20 percent more) effort over time for you to now do in your life to receive those greater 80 percent or more results you want, over any short gap or interval of time now in your life, starting today, by going effortlessly (without any force at all) into a little key 20 percent possession you already have available and very assessable to you called "your own mind." This cosmic 20 percent area or place, which we will referred to as the "The Kingdom" in this book, is the only real cosmic (20 percent) effort you will ever (over any time period in your life) have to perform to surely provide you with those greater results you are now looking to achieve in any area of life. This is the only real 20 percent place or area you will ever have or need to seek, starting henceforth in your life. To surely provide you with those overall greater 80 percent or more results that you've always been seeking to achieve. Yes, those dreams and goals we all have of health, prosperity, happiness, and abundance in our lives.

For you're in essence, via your mind, seeking that key 20 percent thing in your life call "YOU" (The Kingdom) first and foremost, for your dreams in life, and thereafter timeless tangible manifestation. Yes, you will now be seeking that mysterious and key (20 percent) place that you have always over all the time in your life had accessible within you, regardless if you felt you didn't have much else in your life. This is what will now, more so, mysteriously provide you any greater results in any areas of your life over any future time period. This is why you've heard it said in all great philosophy first: "Be true to thy self" (Shakespeare), and "Know thyself" (Socrates).

This again can only be derived by you going quietly and effortlessly (without any force) into your mind first, (The Kingdom) that key 20 percent place, as will be shown to you in this book you're now embarking on. Before everything else in the outside world, your dreams and goals in life can be added to you. This is the reason this book is entitled *Dream It First*, as there has to be a dream first in life, regardless of what else is going on in your life before it can become a full and thereafter physical and tangible manifestation in your life. The effortless task of you now holding this key book in your hands today is definitely a little 20 percent more effort that you or anyone else can use in life. It is an effortless working tool for you to now begin using today to aid you in quickly isolating, identifying, and thereafter using this key and mysterious law to quickly achieve every single dream you ever dreamt all with less of your own efforts.

So, dreamers, let's begin!

HOW THIS MYSTERIOUS LAW WORKS

This mysterious 80/20 Law will work in your life regardless of what your present situations are. It will work regardless of what your past circumstances in life have been, or the cards you may, or may not feel life has inappropriately dealt you. Just know that your dreams will now begin to become an effortless and real manifestation starting today. When you perform the little key 20 percent more effort of unlocking and using the amazing key and invisible "20 percents "nested in all areas of your life that are providing you, mysteriously, those greater 80 percent or more results you want, you can have your heart's desire.

It is, indeed, your innate and God-given right to dream and to have your heart's desire. The key, of course, is to know first what that dream is, found only by going effortlessly first within your key 20 percent place, called your mind. I will now show you in the following chapters, and you will thereafter know what roads to take to manifest those dreams in your life. This book is that road.

SO, DREAMERS, LET'S GET STARTED!

This "80/20" Law indeed is a powerful law that will assist you in achieving more with less of your efforts, including time, worries, emotions, work, money, focus, energy, and any other resources in every single area and aspect of your life, as well as career, family, health, finances, and personal relationships. Because few have discovered the power of this law, they have not been able to apply this silent invisible 80/20 Law in getting all that they truly want, desire, and deserve in life. They have continued to maintain the nightmares of forcing 100 percent of their concerns, emotions, time, money, work, attention, energy, focus, and other resources in life to only achieved little results in what they truly want. This law, as shown earlier, has wonderful properties and benefits. The 80 percent benefits of utilizing this law over time definitely outweigh any 20 percent risk involved, with this information provided. I would like to now devote the remainder of this chapter to the beautiful, invisible, everyday life workings, and discoveries of this law to provide you (now a student of this law) with a fuller knowledge of the powers of this law's qualities, for you will now see this law in full effect.

SO, DREAMERS, LET'S GET READY!

To recap, this powerful law states that approximately 80 percent of your results in life over time will come, or flow from only approximately 20 percent of your efforts. This law also mysteriously implies you indeed will always get more over time with, or using less, meaning that with approximately only 20 percent effort or 80 percent effort you get approximately 80 percent, or 20 percent results of what you are seeking to achieve, or looking not to achieve in life in a shorter or either a longer period of time in your life. It also denotes that "forcing" 100 percent effort in anything is useless in the quest of your dreams, as it provides little results in what you may be looking to achieve (approximately even less than 20 percent results), and that perfection (100 percent in anything) is not needed at all in the quest of your true dreams in life. This law further implies that little is definitely much and much is definitely little, or, worded differently "much is less than and little is much" or either "less than" is "greater than" and "greater than is less than" as shown in the formula illustration here:

> "(<) LESS THAN = GREATER THAN (>)"
>
> "(>) GREATER THAN = LESS THAN (<)"

THE 80/20 LAW IN ACTION

With all the previous information given to you thus far in this chapter, I want you to consider the following facts and factual results, which supports those facts that are applicable and express this law in action over time in your daily life without you being aware of it (as shown below). Did you know that without your awareness and without any of your physical assistance or help at all that over time (approximately) the following things and results are constantly occurring daily in your life:

That only 20 percent of your clothes in your closet are getting 80 percent of the use. That only 20 percent of your carpet in your home will get 80 percent of the wear. That only 20 percent of the rooms in your home over time will get 80 percent of the usage. That 20 percent of the foods in your cabinet over time will get 80 percent of the consumption. That only 20 percent of what you think your soul mate or spouse does not possess in terms of physical attributes, personality, character, or financial status, over time will give or allow you 80 percent of what you do want. Or That 80 percent of what you think your soul mate or spouse does have in the same areas (above) over time will provide, or allow you approximately only 20 percent of what you do want, or need in other areas. This law further implies that the following approximate mysterious results are also occurring in your daily life:

That 80 percent or more of your present or future equity built in your home over time has been built (or will be) built in only 20 percent or less of the time you own your home.

That 80 percent or more of the things you are currently concerned or worried about or you have been concerned or worried about over time only 20 percent or even less has occurred or will ever occur. And that 80 percent or more of all of your frustrations over time have stemmed or is presently stemming from only a 20 percent place, thing, or person in your life. That 80 percent of your business, if you are in business, over time will flow, or come from, only 20 percent of the areas in which you advertise. That 80 percent of your credit over time has or will come from building only 20 percent of your credit. That 80 percent of your overall business, if you are in business, over time will flow directly or indirectly from 20 percent of your present or future customers or clients. That 80 percent of your disposable income over time will be spend on only 20 percent of non-tangible items (such as housing and cars or personal property), and that only 20 percent of that same disposable income over that same time will be spend on 80 percent of your tangible items (such housing cars and other personal property). That 20 percent of your income over time will be spent 80 percent or more in income tax.

That 20 percent or less of your income used to insure everything you own will financially over time off set 80 percent or more of all your future emergences or accidents. That only 20 percent or less of your current income put into a savings over time will provide 80 percent or more of all your present and future financial needs. That 80 percent or more of what you are currently doing or performing right now to change, or modify your child's or spouse's behavior over time will only give you 20 percent or less of the positive results you want, and only 20% or less of what your are currently doing to modify or change that same behavior over time will give you 80 percent or more of the positive results you want. That 80 percent of your friends, family members, employees, or business associates over time will only provide you with 20 percent true friendship, support, or business value. That 80 percent of what physically attracts you to the opposite sex over time will provide you with only 20 percent of what you want, or need. in a good inter-personal relationship. That 80 percent of your daily exercise routine or diet over time will only account for or contribute to only 20 percent of the positive results you're getting, and that only 20 percent of your exercise routine or diet over time will contribute 80 percent or more positive results. That only 20 percent of all the things you are currently doing right now in your life to increase your beauty over time will add 80 percent value. That 80 percent of all things you are performing right now to increase your health or fitness over time will only add 20 percent true value. That 80 percent of all the work being performed on your job or in your business over time will be performed by only 20 percent or less of the employees or staff. That 80 percent of any tasks you are currently working on over time will be completed in only 20 percent of the time you devoted to that task. That 80 percent of all your goals and dreams in life over time will be accomplished in only 20 percent of the time you allot to accomplishing them. Or that 80 percent of your goals in life over time will be accomplished by setting and meeting only 20 percent of those goals. That only 20 percent of your personality over time will attract 80 percent or more of your friends or associates. That only 20 percent or less of all the things you are presently mentally or physically attached to in your life over time will provide you 80 percent or more true value, and that 80 percent or more of the things you are attached to over time will only provide you 20 percent or less value in your life. That only 20 percent of all the qualities, skills, or talents you now possess or will acquire over your life time will account for 80 percent or more of your true successes in life. That only 20 percent of all the things you are currently using to increase your spiritual or personal development over time will provide, or give you, 80 percent value. That just a mere 20 percent more use of your mind or brain over time will provide you with 80 percent or more of all your dreams and goals in life. That with only a 20 percent more effort in any thing you are now working on in life over time will provide you 80 percent or more results, or what appears to be near-perfect results, and finally that even if you are an avid reader, or not, only 20 percent or less of all the books you will read over your life time (as it is with this, and other concisely written books) will truly add 80 percent, or more, value to enrich your life. The results of this law in actions go on and on, and you can prevalently see these mysterious key 20 percents factors playing and affecting every area of our daily lives. You can see these invisible key factors positively as well as negatively, without any effort on your part, affecting your life. This statistical information revealed above simply supports and reveals the fact that little (only 20 percent) of what we do actually control or what we actually do or where we spent our efforts—time, worries, emotions, money, energy, focus, attention, and other resources over the time in our present or past lives—enriches or actually accelerates our dreams and goals." And "largely or mostly of what we do control or where we spent or use 80 percent or more of our efforts—worries, emotions, time, money, focus, energy, attention, or other resources—gives us approximately only 20 percent, or even less. over the present or past times in our lives." With all of this said, the only key and important thing for you to now do in your life, is to start immediately! Continue thereafter isolating and identifying your true key (20 percents) in every single area of your daily life. You must assess the key present and past 20 percent things or key factors that, over intervals of time in your life, has given you more with you using less of all your efforts or has negatively given you less with you using more of all your efforts. This should be done starting today and continued over time throughout the remainder of your life in order for you to turbo-boost all your intended dreams and goals in life. Once you have isolated and identified those key mysteriously 20 percent factors (things, people, and areas) in your life that has given or is currently giving you (directly or indirectly) the greater results of what you want you want to immediately start putting your entire weight and efforts (faith, thoughts, work, beliefs, emotions, time, money, energy, attention, and other resources) only on those key things, people or areas in your life that over time has given you more! Not less. You will henceforth starting today alleviate not having any tolerance (any longer) for all those other people, areas, or things in yourself and in your life that has actually worked over time to provide you less. You, despite your fear, feeling, or emotions towards the outcome must now stop all affects that for any period of time over your life that has not given you more of what you want now only accommodating those key people, things, or areas in your life, as well as in yourself, that giving you more over shorter or longer intervals of time in your life. You will now no longer devote any of your focus or efforts—your time, worries, emotions, concerns, beliefs, actions, thoughts, work, energy, attention, money, or any other of your resources—if you have not done so up to this point in your life, you have definitely over time in your life been "getting much less with much more" over longer as well as shorter intervals of time over the time in your life without your awareness. This is the great hidden

mystery of this powerful and beautiful "80/20 Law." For example (regarding your finances), if you have just quickly
mentally isolated and observed in your own mind from the
all the recent statistics just revealed earlier that a key 20 percent and significant portion of your present or past income
has indeed been paid heavenly (approximately 80 percent or
more) in (income) taxes over the past recent years in your
life—due to the lack of income tax exemptions you're presently carrying or have carried in recent years. This without
your possible awareness, indeed, has definitely negatively affected the net and key amount of money you bring home on
your bi-monthly pay check. If you have identified this key
and important factor as such in your own personal life from
reading this book, you definitely want to now become an astute 80/20 thinker in this lesser, yet key and important 20
percent area and key factor in your life. Simply by you now
putting more of your emphasis on this little key area in your
life and off other key areas that has been (mysteriously) de-
ferring you from turbo-bursting many of your other dreams
and goals in life. You acting as though this key and vital and
20 percent area or factor you have just identified above isn't
gravely affecting your life or your overall goals and dreams,
as well as your overall income. You "forcing" your physical
efforts by working longer hours or over time hours on your
present job is not the ostensible answer! This, believe it or
not, will only "force" and cause you over time in your life to
pay even more personal income tax in this same key 20 percent area by you now simply "lessening" this key 20 percent
area all together. By you simply doing what most other 80/20
thinkers, as well as what approximately 20 percent of the
population is now effortlessly doing or has done in the past
in this key area over time you will get more, This is done by
you investing your pre-tax or before tax earning in key things
in your life that will reduce or totally delete that key 20 percent area all together (as well as produce income for you),
not by forcing and having more children only to solve part of
the problem which may only increase those tax exemption

(know as dependents) on your paycheck (yet produces no income), which some may think is the only likely solution, but by you simply effortlessly stepping out of your own present fears and/or comfort zone and perhaps your own "limited thinking." Consider a little 20 percent calculated risk of investing in things key things in your life like buying a home or even more real property, owning your own full or part-time business, donating a portion of your income to a church or other nonprofit organization that personally inspires and serves you, or consider investing your pre-tax or before tax money in deferred saving plans, tax annuities, or other tax deferred vehicles. Any of these few, yet key things (explained professionally to you in full detail by your tax advisor) will allow you to immediately increase those current tax exemptions you carry on your next paycheck, allowing you to give yourself an instant raise! This will also allow you to keep more or possibly all of that key 20 percent you would have, otherwise, paid in income taxes. All this by you simply lessening a vital key (20 percent) area in your life that over time and for too long in your life has given you, not more, but less of what you want in life! Using this key approach you're be able to now quickly accelerate and leverage even more greater dreams and goals in your life!

For those readers who are presently in business you may easily relate to the following illustration, which again reveals this powerful 80/20 law in full action: If you are utilizing several avenues in your business for advertisement, if you took just a mere 20 percent more of your time to assess the results of your advertisement by polling all your customers or clients to determine how they heard about your business, you would easily see that approximately 80 percent of your customers or clients are coming directly or indirectly from only approximately 20 percent of what you're doing in your marketing and advertisement efforts, not from all of your 100 percent efforts.

If you had an advertisement in your local newspaper, on a commercial bench advertisement, in your local phone book, and you were also passing out business cards, and business flyers, as well as providing exceptional service to all your current customers and clients as an advertisement campaign to increase your business revenue, and if you would over a considerable "time," say one year, perform an immediate analysis at the end of your campaign, you could clearly see where the greater percentage of your business was actually coming from. You could easily assess that approximately only 20 percent or less of your business is truly coming from the (above) 100 percent areas in which you are advertising, and that approximately 80 percent or more of your business is actually coming from only an approximately 20 percent or less area in which you are advertising. Before I became fully aware of the power of this "80/20 Law," we had done quite a bit of advertisement for the legal document and paralegal business that I own. Over a period of time we were able to clearly identify, by our office using and employing this 80/20 law, that approximately 80 percent or more of our business was really flowing directly from only three of our advertisement sources. In our case, this was a bench advertisement in front of our business, an illuminated sign that stayed lighted in our window twenty-four hours, and the exceptional good service that we were providing to all of our current clients and customers visiting our office. By our office simply isolating and identifying these three lesser (20 percent) areas out of all the 100 percent areas and places we had advertised in, it not only saved us money—to the tune of thousands of advertisement dollars each year—but it also saved us time and energy as well in all of our advertisement efforts! It literally deleted all our advertisement costs, as we no longer had to use all the other 80 percent areas we were currently using or had previously used.

The one-time cost that we accrued in the purchase of the bench ad outside our business, and the commercial window sign along with the little required time and effort of providing exceptional good service to our current clients and customers (which required no monetary efforts at all) had given us an approximate 80 percent or more return on our initial approximate 20 percent financial investment only over a short time period. We were immediately able to see that the three lesser areas or places our business had advertised in had, indeed, given us our greater results, despite us not fully understanding "how or when" it all occurred. I now not only use this powerful "80/20" Law in all my professional business endeavors as shown above, but in every other area in my life—personal, financial, and otherwise—anywhere I'm looking to achieve greater results using less of my time, money, attention, energy, and other efforts in any shorter gap or period of time. I have definitely become an adept and skillful "80/20 Thinker," "always getting more in shorter gaps of time over my life," not a careless and unskilled "20/80 thinker" "getting less of what I want over longer intervals of time in my life," as I will now show you how to become in the following pages.

Again, once any key 20 percent is identified that's providing you the greater results of what you really want in shorter intervals of time in any area of your life, using less time or other efforts, you want to immediately stop putting any emphasis on those other areas and start only putting your entire weight, emphasis, or start having tolerance only on those lesser key 20 percent areas or things only that are giving you your greater results in a short gap of your time over your life (as shown below).

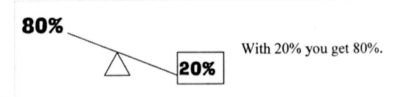

With 20% you get 80%.

You will henceforth in your life alleviate all your previous efforts, time, concentrations, and force in all the 100 percent areas or things that have truly only provided you with approximately 20 percent, or even less, of what you want in life, and you will now only put weight (as illustrated above) on the 20 percent areas or things that have provided, or is providing, you the greater 80 percent or more of what you want, for you will definitely be getting more with less in a much shorter gap of time over your life, for you now know that "much" of is really "less of."

Identifying the invisible key and central 20 percent areas or things in your life that are providing you your greater results over time using less of your resources is the real key to quickly unleashing and turbo-boosting any enlightened dreams in your life with little effort. This, believe it or not, will happen without little conscious or physical effort on your part, as the invisible unknown spiritual components of this law will go to work on your behalf, again, without your assistance.

This effortless task of identifying and using the central or key 20 percent areas or things in your life to "achieve" more with less in shorter lengths of time in your life has consciously, as well as unconsciously, been used by countless of successful individuals in manifesting their true dreams in life. This has happened often without their full awareness, in areas of better and increased personal and inter-personal relationships, better health, career, finances, and overall abundance in their lives, simply because somewhere in their own picture they were using less or more of something consciously or unconsciously identified as their personal key (20 percent) in a particular area of their lives to obtain more by using less over time in their lives. This has happened in their lives often without their awareness, as depicted here in the following story. A very close business friend of mine, after learning about this mysterious law revealed in this book, related to me that he had, in fact, without his own awareness at the time, had indeed used this 80/20 law over a previous gap of time in his own life to realize an enlightened dream that for many years was out of reach for him. This was for him to quickly, in some effortless way, accumulate wealth and financial independences.

When growing up in a small suburban town in Alexander, Louisiana, he, along with his three brothers and parents, resided in a modest thirteen hundred square feet, ten-room home, which consisted of three bedrooms, two baths, a kitchen (that included a nook), a living room, dining room a family room, and an exterior laundry room. Yet, he found himself throughout his youth living at home comfortably only using approximately 20 percent of those ten rooms, which included his bedroom, the bathroom, and kitchen. After moving to Los Angeles, California as an adult, he said it only made sense for him to continue with what had previously worked well for him in his life. He decided to rent (which deviated from the norm of what everyone else was doing) a small studio apartment. This area that he rented, believe it or not, consisted of the same three rooms he had effortlessly and comfortably occupied as a youth growing up in his home town: a living room (which doubled as a bedroom), kitchen, and bath. He related to me that by him leveraging these key 20 percent living areas over an extended gap of time in his life he now sees how he was able to comfortably live on and in this lesser (approximately 20 percent) area, yet, still over time, without any effort as well as to accumulate wealth, while he used the money he would have otherwise spent over time on increase furnishing, utilities, maintenance, rent/mortgage and other more expensive lifestyle amenities that he really did not need. This, he revealed, in fact, would have "forced" him to spend much more money, as well as other resources over time, for a larger and much more expensive apartment or house. He related that after he had worked to acquired his real estate broker's licenses (and begin to produce income part time from that capacity) he was then able to quickly leverage the increased income he made but he did not need, to support his "lesser" and "below means" lifestyle, and to purchase several rental properties in California's deflated real estate market, which he then effortlessly in a short time rented out to people displaced by that same deflated market. This alone gave him a positive liquid (monthly) cash flow, and ultimately within a short three-month period of time afterwards turbo burst and thereafter tripled his net worth several times over, which not only gave him wealth, but financial stability. All this occurred with little of his own efforts, and in a much shorter time then he thought despite him not fully understanding how or when it had all actually happened. All this timelessly and effortlessly manifested while he still (over time) continued to live in those same lesser key (20 percent) areas in his apartment he had not then identified. Yet, they indeed over time in his life, without his awareness, provided him "much more by using less of something else in his life." This again is the great beauty and hidden mystery of this invisible spiritual 80/20 law.

I have been a licensed real estate and mortgage broker for the past twenty-one years and have shared with a myriad of my clients the power in levering this key and powerful 80/20 law when buying real estate, as depicted in the following analogy: When a residential lender or bank pre-qualifies a buyer for a home mortgage, they may not always reveal that they are actually qualifying them for the largest or maximum loan mortgage payment that they can possibly afford not the smaller or lesser payment they could possibly afford. This is based solely on approximately thirty percent or one-third of their total monthly gross income. This qualifying ratio does not include any of their monthly household bills or expenses; the bank now considers this factor as their "front end" debt to loan ratio. Yet, their total monthly living expenses and bills alone with their proposed future mortgage payment (should not exceed approximately forty percent or one-quarter of their total gross income in the bank's calculations) is a factor that the bank considers the buyer's "back end" debt to loan buying ratio. The buyer's new total (front and back) loan to debt ratio is (now) a simple key factor and equation of what's referred to in the banking industry as "30/40." A key factor and equation that most banks will use or consider as their own "conforming loan" standard or guideline to identify and determine (not the buyer's financial risk) their own financial risk in making their proposed loan to a potential buyer. If any potential home buyer would simply deviate from this eighty percent buying "norm" or practice, which is what most or approximately eighty percent or more of what most home buyers have done when buying a home (as shown above). Simply consider buying or getting a much "smaller home mortgage" "less than" those "30/40" ratios their bank recommends, by considering a much smaller mortgage or buying ratio of only twenty to twenty-five percent ("front end") ratio. For example, buy in a total lower (front and back end ratio) range of "20/30" or "25/35." This is easily accomplished, believe it or, not by the buyer simply purchasing a smaller or less expensive home (within these approximate "20/30" or '25/35' ratios), but by the buyer simply purchasing a smaller home (yet buying it in a more superior location or neighborhood) than they could have afforded the more expensive home in that same superior location. By using this key 80/20 real estate approach to home buying, they would be simply levering way more in this key "20 percent" area over time, as well as leveraging and increasing more of their own buying power and decreasing their own personal financial risk, all by simply using this 80/20 law's approach. With this effortless, yet key method, they'll actually accumulate faster equity over a shorter period of time than they would have over a longer period of time by simply buying a larger or more expensive home in a more inferior neighborhood within those ratios recommended by their bank. Using this effortless yet, key approach any home buyer over time would be able to quickly accumulated cash equity (with that smaller home) that would soon enable them to put a much larger down payment on a larger home in that same superior, or even better neighborhood or location. What they have automatically done over time was "off set and leverage" their own present and future personal wealth as well as their own financial risk for any possible future unexpected changes in their personal "incoming," or "outgoing" income, which in itself could easily "force" anyone having to make a large mortgage payment in the event their incoming or outgoing income negatively or abruptly changed, as seen so much with many in today's economy. The (conscious) unawareness of this key (80/20) approach when buying real estate is what has largely contributed to the large percentage of foreclosures we see in today' s real estate economy and market where buyers have gotten ostensibly "more" (with more larger mortgages and more larger homes) yet over time has received much less. This effortless (80/20) approach to home ownership is a key method to permanent home ownership for anyone, all by one simply isolating, identifying, and then lessening a key 20 percent factor in their present lives.

To further illustrate another hidden and unknown mystery as well as a great personal benefit anyone will derive in using this 80/20 Law in their own personal life. I'll share the following observations in my own personal life: I am hardly perfect and I have to admit that I personally have not always been a very health conscious person. I have to admit that I do possess some fairly bad habits, which doesn't merit healthy living by anyone's standards! Still, I have been able over time to manage these apparent weaknesses in my personal life by using more of some other key and important 20 percents factors that have indeed over the time in my life been working to counter those apparent weaknesses, even without my awareness. They have actually given me more over longer periods of time in my life, although I'll done less in other areas of my life. Believe it or not, many people have constantly asked me "time and time again" how have I apparently, without giving much effort at all, been able to maintain over time my youthful appearance, apparent good health, as well as my "beauty" for my fifty-plus age. A few key (20 percents) that I have recently personally isolated and then identified for myself by using this 80/20 law's approach has apparently worked continuously well for me over the time in my life. It has helped me maintain my (less than ten years my actual age) appearance, non-prescription drug use, and hospitalizations (aside from childbirth). I have over a longer than shorter period of time during my life been an avid high quantity water, vitamin, and dietary supplement consumer, and I have maintained this effortless (unconscious) regimen alone with an effortless no pork meat diet for over the past 30 years. These few things in conjunction with my happily keeping myself active, as well as quite busy performing my daily personal and business endeavors have proven over time, even without my awareness, to be my true keys! I can now personally vouch for these few effortless things that I surprisingly just recently isolated and then identified in my own life. I have personally discerned from this that these few little key things over time in my life has always been there and has served as my personal little keys that I have unconsciously used. They have allowed me to achieve and maintain my health, my weight, as well as my "beauty" at my age. I have unconsciously used these few yet key elements in maintaining my health and youthful appearance all without using very little of anything else or other efforts in terms of money, time, or other resources in my life. As a key result of this of course! I have never had to put emphasis on (or deny myself the pleasure) forcing and using other non-effective, restrictive, costly, and time-consuming, health or beauty regimens. I've been able to freely and simply live my life without forcing any of those constraints. This is another beautiful key benefit you or anyone else will always personally receive by now using this mysterious 80/20 Law.

Another (yet) surprising personal key (20 percent) that I've recently identified in my own home that most women may easily relate to involves my white carpet. I recently found out (over time) that the white carpet in my home wasn't actually giving more overall of what I really wanted, but much less. By simply using this 80/20 law's approach I was able to quickly isolate by observation that approximately only 20 percent or less of my white carpet in my home over time had gotten about 80 percent or more of the actual use. This small yet regularly used key area over time had accumulated a lot of built in grime, dirt, and uneven wear. This painstaking end result had taken and used up much of my time, attention, as well as my frustrations over the previous years. I had many failed attempts in keeping this small yet, regularly used key area as clean and evenly worn as the other 80 percent carpeted areas in my home. Once I identified that this little yet, key negative thing and key factor in my life was causing me much of my frustrations, as well as unproductive use of time, I got rid of (not all) the white carpet, which I actually liked. I simply got rid of and then replaced those key (20 Percent) and lesser few areas that were getting all the dirt, grime, and wear, because they were actually being walked on 80 percent or more of the time, with hardwood flooring. This instantly solved my problem, allowing me to still keep my white carpet and have much more time for other things too! I was able over time to keep more money I had regularly spent for professional carpet cleaning and also more of my own personal time. I also alleviated my frustrations by not having to regularly clean or constantly have visitors remove their shoes. This has instantly allowed me much more happiness and even more time to focus on way more important things in my life, all while still beautifully maintaining my home, as well as my carpet, the way I like. All this effortlessly happened by me simply isolating, identifying, and then using "less of" this hidden key 20 percent thing in my life that for too long over time in my life was actually giving me much less of what I really wanted yet, using way more of my efforts.

HOW TO BECOME AN 80/20 THINKER

In order to achieve maximum benefit and leverage from the use of this powerful "80/20 Law" in manifesting any real dream in your life, you, in truth, will need to become a skilled conscious "80/20 Thinker," not an unconscious "80/20 Thinker," as with my dear friend earlier. You will not only need to become an ongoing skilled and conscious "80/20 Thinker" in some areas of your life, but in every single area of your life—starting today. This is really not hard to do at all, as it only takes an approximately 20 percent more effort in the things you're currently doing in your life. All you must be willing to do is simply be able to isolate, observe, and identify those key (20 percent) things, people, or areas in yourself and in your life that's providing you or has in the past provided you more of what you want with you using less of your efforts, time, worries, emotions, money, energy, or other resources. Once those key 20 percent areas or things in your life and in yourself have been identified, you thereafter will only need to start or continue putting your entire emphasis only on those key things identified by simply doing more in that 20 percent area or more of that thing you have identified and taking your efforts off those key things you have identified that's giving you less. This is easily accomplished by you then putting your entire weight on or only having tolerance for those key 20 percent areas, things, or people in your life that you have identified, not on all the other 80 percent areas (things or people) in your life, which has actually provided you less of what you're seeking to receive using more of your efforts over long periods of time. The following simple guideline, and story that accompanies it, is an easy tool you can start using today in your life to begin effortlessly isolating and identifying those key or central 20 percents invisibly nested in any area of your life.

SO, DREAMERS, LET'S GET STARTED!

FIVE STEPS TO QUICKLY ISOLATING AND IDENTIFING YOUR PRESENT OR PAST) KEY (20 PERCENT) THINGS AND PEOPLE IN YOUR LIFE.

1. Isolate and I.D. what it is that you presently want, or I.D. or isolate what it was you wanted in the past.
2. Determine the methods (things in yourself) or (things or people) you will presently use or I.D. those same

methods (things or people) you have previously used in the past.

3. Observe the methods (things or people) you will presently use or I.D. the methods (things or people) you have previously observed in the past.
4. Allow time to lapse, or I.D. the time you have previously allowed to lapse in the past)
5. Evaluate your results.

THE RESULTS

The smaller or fewer methods in yourself or in the things or people isolated and then identified to you, over any period of time you have allowed to lapse in your life of all the total sum of all the methods, things, or people you have used, regardless of how odd or illogical they appear to you, are the mysterious key 20 percent areas in yourself or in the things or people in your life that have nevertheless presently allowed or is presently disallowing you your greater results, or has previously over the past time in your life allowed or has disallowed you your greater 80 percent or more results in your life. Again, this rings true regardless of you not knowing how and when it has occurred or your emotional feeling towards these true end results. A while back during the time I was operating my board and care facilities for developmentally disabled consumers, I had hired a "perfect" employee that came highly recommended for the ideal salary I could afford to pay her, and her exceptional past work experience and a very flexible work schedule could greatly benefit our clients. Prior to my hiring this "ostensible key person," things had been running smoothly within our daily business operation. Yet, I observed almost immediately (within a short two week period) after hiring her for some unknown, yet key reason, things seemed to "go south" in my business. I wasn't quite able to consciously figure out or pinpoint just what was causing all the new upset in our business, and neither could the other present staff members. The only little thing that I could tell had slightly changed at that time was my new addition of this "key" person to our team. Confused, I quickly put this 80/20 law's approach to work! By my simply using the above five steps outlined earlier as my guide, I was able to isolate, observe, and ID that the new employee was indeed the lesser or smaller of the things I had recently done in my business. After making my list of the things I wanted in my business, I was able to quickly isolate and then ID, after my close observation of this employee, over a short one-month period all the key things she was indeed adding to our business, as well as the key things she apparently wasn't adding. By my doing this I could clearly see that that she was, in fact, giving our business far less benefits over just this short length of time of her employment with a much longer list (over that same time period) of problems that didn't benefit my business at all. Despite my initial good and emotional feeling towards this employee, as well as the ostensible economical benefits I thought she could have brought to our business, I quickly made the decision to terminate her employment, as I had definitely gotten far less with more problems with this "key" employee. I quickly discerned that the risk of keeping her on as an employee definitely outweighed the benefits she had or could bring to our business. Had I not quickly used this key 80/20 approach, she indeed over time would have caused our business much more long-term problems. Without your awareness, your physician or mental healthcare professionals you may use are all consciously or unconsciously using this 80/20 approach (outlined above) to identify and isolate a key (20 percent) medication or regimen used to cure most of your physical, mental pain, or medical issues as shown in the following story. You may finally decide to visit your doctor for a chronic illness, for which you may have used the previous months concurrently exhausting all of your own home methods or remedies to cure. You may even provide your doctor a list of all the things you have tried. Your doctor, after assessing your needs and your acute symptoms, simply prescribes one (the lesser) of those medications or regimen you have been using and gives you strict instructions to follow. He may inform you to stop taking or using all other medications and regimens you have previously used (by him telling you this he is simply isolating that particular medication or regimen). He will then allow adequate time to lapse to evaluate the results, telling you, "I'll see you again in two weeks." When you do return after this short, two-week recommended period of time, you happily inform the doctor that the medication or regimen that he prescribed has worked very well for you over this short time period. What he has actually done, with this key information you have provided him, is to "evaluate your results." He now tells you to continue taking only that one medication or use that one regimen, so you begin to live your life free of that particular physical or mental pain or illness. "Presto!" That medication or regimen identified is now your "key" medication or regimen to use, simply because he has isolated that one key medication or regimen and subsequently determined if it is your key medication or regimen to use to cure your particular illness. Of course! With this new found information, you now only take that one medication or use only that one regimen, and you stop taking or using all the other methods, medication, or regimens you may had previously used for that same pain or illness, which has not over time given you more (in a shorter period of time) of the positive results or greater results you wanted with you using less of all of your efforts. All this has happened simply by your doctor isolating and then identifying that key 20 percent (medication or regiment) especially for you.

The great spiritual mystery of and behind this 80/20 Law is that how or when the results are manifested over time is not fully understood; nevertheless, the results are factual and of use to us in accelerating and turbo-boosting any of our dreams and goals in life. This all denotes the spiritual or invisible working components of this "anti-force," yet powerful law, as I will further discern to you in the following story illustrations below.

As I related earlier in the book's introduction, I'm a business and motivational speaker. I also occasionally consult as a personal life coach with some of my attendees in my audience or with those who visit my website. Mary, one of my consultants who's a very independent matter-of-fact-type business woman, admitted to me on several occasions that she was not a very "spiritual-minded" person, as she called it. She needed to see the real and tangible bare results and facts that lead to those results in everything in her life. However, reluctantly, in one or our coaching sessions, she did reveal to me that she had tried everything (given 100 percent effort) (call force) and was still experiencing on-going frustrations over the past several years in finding a potential and suitable spouse/soul mate that possessed 100 percent of the qualities that she felt she really needed in a mate. I, randomly, in one of our ongoing conversations, informed Mary that she may want to approach her objective of finding a suitable mate by using the little (key) effort of simply isolating the key things or areas in the men she was currently dating to "ID" if they were actually providing her more or the greater results of what she wanted in a more timely fashion using less of her efforts, yet not possibly giving her all the 100 percent results or key things she only felt she needed in a mate. Mary reluctantly agreed that this suggestion (although she didn't fully understand it) did make sense to her, as she had nothing else to lose in trying it, since everything she had tried thus far over time in the past several years had only eaten up her time and hadn't given her close to any of the positive results she wanted. I offered Mary the general outline (shown above) to follow. To facilitate Mary in accomplishing these steps indicated in the outline, I followed the outline along with Mary as indicated here:

STEP #1 from the above outline: "I.D. or isolate what it is you now want" (or have wanted in the past). Mary simply isolated and identified all the attributes and qualities that she felt she now needed and had to have in any mate. Mary decided to accomplish this task by making the following list below, so she could refer to it later. Mary's list consisted of having a man in her life that was:

Generous*
Warm*
Good at communicating
Neat in appearance*
Romantic
Handsome*
Family oriented*
Professional*
Humorous*
Financially Stable*

STEP #2 from the above outline: "Determine the method(s) (people or things) you will use" (or you have used in the past.) Mary accomplished this step by deciding to use Rodney, the man she had been dating for the past six months, as her "method" to see if he displayed any of the qualities she wanted (in Step #1).

STEP #3 from the above outline: "Observe the method (people or things) you will use" (or you have used in the past). Mary observed the method (Rodney) by continuing her present dating of him, whom she had already been dating for the past six months.

STEP #4 from the above outline: "Allow adequate time to lapse," or (ID the time you have allowed to lapse in the past). Mary accomplished this next step by deciding to date Rodney for an additional six months. Mary allowed this second six-month period to lapse, as she felt this was adequate (time) for her to collect, evaluate, and analyze all her results.

STEP #5 from the outline: "Evaluate your results": Mary then evaluated and analyzed the results collected from her list she had made, as shown in Step #1.

MARY'S RESULTS

Mary analyzed her ten-item list to determine if Rodney elicited or displayed the type of dream attributes/qualities she desired simply isolating those areas on her list by putting an asterisk next to all the attributes on the list that Rodney did possess, and then isolating the other areas by highlighting those on the list he did not possess, as shown above. Because Mary did this, she could vividly see that Rodney did not possess two desired qualities or things, which she always felt she just had to have in any mate. These two things actually represented only 20 percent of all the things on her ten-item list. One, he did not have very good communication skills, and two, he was not very romantic. Mary, using the guidelines above, was able to vividly see that 20 percent of the items or things on her list (two out of the ten items), the two smaller or lesser areas or things, Rodney did not possess, but nevertheless, he did have all that she did want in the other remaining 80 percent areas on her list. The 20 percent that he did not possess was, indeed, without her understanding how had, in fact, allowed her over time to have exactly 80 percent of what she wanted overall in the remaining other 80 percent areas on her list. "Presto!" She, in fact, had gotten way "more with less." All this happened in a shorter period of time than she has previously devoted to this painstaking quest. With this information, and new defining knowledge, Mary continued to pursue her relationship with Rodney, and a year later accepted his proposal of marriage. She had discerned that her previous efforts of trying to get 100 percent of all the qualities she wanted in a man had not served her true objective or goal of finding a suitable mate who would give her more of all the things she wanted in a shorter length of time with her using less of her "know-how," time, or other efforts. She had to assert that she indeed had "gotten much more with much less," or to be put another way "she had gotten way more in a shorter period of time, of what she wanted by taking less of something else she only emotionally felt she needed." All this, of course, happened without her fully understanding how or when, again, the great hidden mystery of this mysterious spiritual 80/20 Law.

This same outline used above is also applicable in identifying the key 20 percent areas or things that are not allowing or disallowing you your greater results as well. For example, if Mary had found, by using the same five steps above, that Rodney (out of the ten items on her list) had only possessed, or elicited two isolated qualities representing only 20 percent of the qualities on her list that she only felt she really needed, only having good communication skills and being romantic, these two lesser (20 percent) areas or things isolated and identified would have, believe it or not, been the "key 20 percent" things on her list that were *not* providing her more over a short interval of time or giving her 80 percent of what she wanted (her greater results) in the other 80 percent areas (as shown in the earlier illustration with the "other women" in the movie *Why Did I Get Married*). In this case, these results would have indicated that Rodney was not a very good and suitable mate for her, as she had not received more, but less of her true objective or goal over a longer period of time. In fact, she would have gotten way more of what she did not want over a longer period of time with less of what she did want in the same length of time.

Sometimes en route to our dreams in life, we don't even dare to isolate, look at, or assess in our minds all the key things in ourselves, as well as in our life that may surely appear or does not possibly appear to us as our ostensible key 20 percent things in our lives that has given us more or less. Maybe because of their earlier emotional or economic deposits, or either their non emotional or economic deposits made into our lives. Maybe because of our unconscious fear and anxiety of what our assessing these key areas in ourselves, as well as in our lives, would or could bring to our own awareness. All again because of our present emotional/economical, or our non emotional/economical bonds to those ostensible key things in ourselves, or in the key people or things in our lives. Perhaps, it's a combination of

all three of these things. Believe it or not regardless of our
key reasons, these key areas, despite our fears or reasoning,
has to also on going in our lives be isolated and identified
in order to begin and continue thereafter effortlessly turbo-
boosting our true dreams in life. We must assess all ostensible "key things including ourselves and the other people in
our lives" to determine and or to affirm if they or you have
actually given you more or less in a shorter or either longer
time frames over your life using more or less of all of our
resources and efforts as shown earlier. If they have actually
added or given you more of what you want (by using the
five steps above as a guide line), this will just be an affirming and added realization that they (or you) are the true key
(methods) people or things in your life. If by using the same
above five steps you assess (as shown in the above case with
Mary), they, as well as yourself, are actually not the method,
providing you less with you using more of your efforts or
resources over a long or longer period of time in your life,
then this is also a sure and key realization that they or yourself are "not" actually the "key people," "methods" or things
that you may have thought or felt they were. They or you, as
hard as it may be for you to believe, are presently (although
perhaps in the past they had given you more) is now giving
you less not more over the present time in your life. If this
is the case, despite your emotional bond, your weight must
be immediately lifted and taken off those key things in yourself, as well as off the people and things that have, in fact,
given you less over a, not shorter but, a longer length of time
in your life. If you or anyone else would take the effortless
time (of using this powerful key 20 percent effort) as shown
earlier with the case of Mary, they too would positively assert the same, as Mary did in the story above, that they're
definitely getting more positive results in shorter intervals of
time in their lives with less pain, frustrations, time, money,
energy, attention, or other efforts, or either they'll assert the
opposite that they have gotten less of the same. For those
dreamers who are reading this book and are already utiliz-

ing this powerful and key law, I'm sure you would agree that you have definitely seen over short intervals or gaps of time over your life in many cases where you have used this law, and that this key 20 percent effort of isolating and identifying for yourself the key 20 percent things (in yourself), the people and areas in everything (past or even presently in your life) has provided your greater results, with you using little of your own efforts. As a result of this, I'm sure you no longer utilize all the other 80 percent methods, things, or people in your life or in yourself that have actually over time given you less of what you want. This book, for those who do fall into this uncanny category, is just an indication that you may be what others may refer to as that "esoteric" 20 percent of lucky people that many see from afar, as that "special group" of people in the world, but you're really not! What you really are is an 80/20 Thinker! You are definitely, what appears to the world, someone who's part of a special 20 percent group in the population that's definitely getting 80 percent, or more, of what they want in life in short intervals of time over their lives with only an approximately 20 percent, or less, effort.

One of the many personal reasons I have written this book is for a longer than shorter portion of my life I would say I have been (what I now see myself as) "an astute 80/20 Thinker" in many areas of my life. I have definitely (over the time in my life without being aware of it) used this mysterious 80/20 Law to my advantage in my life. To isolate, observe, and then I.D. not the larger things but the smaller key things in myself as well as the key things in my life that was giving me more not less using less of all of my efforts or resources. This is what has truly allowed me to accomplish so many concurrent and multiple dreams over such small interval and gaps of time over my life, despite the concurrent nightmares in my life. At times, I would question myself, because I would often see myself doing little key imperfect things that deviated from the "norm" of what everyone else was doing, as previous shown with my dear friend from Louisiana. Often, I would be ridiculed over time in my life, for not doing things the same as everyone else, by those 80 percent masses in my life. What I now of course know, and have recognized, is that this so-called "norm," or the greater masses in the world, is really the 80 percent group in the world that are not, apparently, getting to or even achieving or accelerating many of their enlightened dreams, and goals in their lives, for they are not utilizing this 80/20 law to its fullest, or most likely they're not using it at all.

You see, when one is utilizing this powerful yes spiritual 80/20 law in their lives, they are no longer trying to be "perfect" like everyone else or part of the greater masses in the world today. They're truly no longer a part of the 100 percent population. They are astute "20 percenters" and "80/20 Thinkers." They're the "Real Effortless Dreamers" you see in the world living their personal dreams. If you find yourself as well as anyone else in life forcing and doing 100 percent of what everyone else is doing, you must now know that this, in itself, has to be a huge indication to you that you're probably not on the right key track. If you were, why aren't 100 percent or all of the "perfect" people in the world, effortlessly, living and turbo-boosting their true dreams?

By you now just putting 20 percent more effort in stepping out of your old fear and old "comfort zone," your old 100 percent (negative) effort ways of doing things, you will now begin to effortlessly arrive at your dreams in life. This, of course, may feel a little uncomfortable to you initially, for if there is 100 percent in our population and only 20 percent is doing the needed 20 percent preparation for their 80 percent dreams in their lives, one can easily feel a little uncomfortable and lonely, at first. But know that in your quest for your dreams you'll be utilizing, as we will be discussing in later chapters, another powerful 20 percent and key element, called "The Law of Attraction," where you will indeed over time attract other "20 percenters" and "80/20 Thinkers" in your life, as well as great comfort and your wonderful enlightened dreams in a shorter periods of time in your life.

You are now utilizing spiritual law! To manifest all of your real dreams and goals in your life, and the definition of any spiritual law is that it does or cannot fail you! It has been proven over time beyond a doubt only when the mythology and the philosophy behind the law's mythology are applied, as has been explained and shown to you in this chapter. Even if you haven't been putting your entire weight on or off those small key 20 percent negative areas and key things in yourself, as well as the other people and things in your life over the previous or past intervals of time in your life, don't worry. By you now by using this mysterious and fertile 80/20 law's approach in every area of your life, henceforth, you can still over time "finish up maybe last" not with less, but more! This is the hidden mystery of this law. With your now defining knowledge of this mysterious 80/20 spiritual law that's now been isolated, identified, and discerned to you here in this chapter, you, starting today, will no longer have to be concerned with the 100 percent stuff in the world. You'll simply just stay focused on those key 20 percent areas in yourself, as well as the other key people and things that you have personally identified in your life that's presently providing you the greater of what you want of your dreams and goals. This is the only real 20 percent more effort you will ever need to do to now in life to take you effortlessly to any of your dreams. This will happen now with you only taking a mere 20 percent more effort of whatever you're doing now!

SO, DREAMERS, LET'S GET STARTED!

THE 80/20 SILENT MESSAGE

The silent message revealed in this mysterious spiritual "80/20 Law" that you have just explored is that little of what we actually do over, or in, the time of our lives, or where we spend most of all of our focus and efforts, like time, worries, money, energy, work, emotions, or other resources (only approximately 20 percent) actually over any time gap in our lives (especially the gap of time prior to our dreams mani-festing) enriches our lives, or truly helps us in reaching our intended dreams in life. This key and important gap of time in our lives from the time of a stimulus of any dream in our lives to the time of that dream's final physical manifestation or the final response to that stimulus is simply termed: The key gap of time between the "stimulus and the response" a gap that we must surely effectively use en route to any of our dreams and goals in life. What we do or where we put any of our resources (our faith time, money, work, emotions, energy, focus, attention, thoughts, or our other efforts) over and during this key and important gap of time in our lives, prior to our dreams manifesting will be the key 20% cause that will provide and give us our greater key 80 percent or more effects or results of what we desire or do not desire in life. Now that you know that acknowledging and only putting your entire emphasis only on those few and key 20 percent things personally identified in yourself, during this present and important key gap of time now in your life, because they will personally provide you your greater results over a shorter interval of time now in your life. You can indeed un-lock the enormous and amazing potential of all those other "key 20 percent" things, invisibly nested in all areas of your life, thereafter, more quickly multiplying and turbo-boosting all your dreams and goals of health, prosperity, happiness, and abundance in your life.

The key time that you (or anyone else) must surely allow to lapse, (during this now important and key gap of time now in your life till your dreams are manifested) allowing you time to personally isolate, observe, and identify for yourself all those fertile and cosmos key things presently invisibly nested within you, does not over time have to be person-ally spent or used by you. They've already been spent and used, especially for you, already. The spiritual laws and the only real key "mind" that governs those key laws will bring forth every intended dream in every single area of your life will now be beautifully, lawfully, and effortlessly unfolded and identified to you in the remaining chapters. These spiritual laws over time have been isolated, identified and now revealed, as the cosmic (20 percent) keys invisibly nested and readily available, not only in my life, but every single person's life. When your full and entire weight and emphasis is now effortlessly put only on these few key laws during this now present gap of time in your life until your dreams are finally manifested they will quickly begin to effortlessly turbo-boost all your individual dreams and goals of health, prosperity, and abundance in your life. These laws have been identified as the only key spiritual laws to all health, prosperity, and abundance in every area of your life not only by me, but by countless other successful "80/20 Thinkers" and successful "Dreamers" in life who have over time effortlessly used these key "anti-force" still, powerful laws to conquer personal nightmares and begin turbo-boosting their enlightened dreams into existence. By you now using this short and present key gap of time now in your life, you will see your dreams begin to quickly manifest at the accelerated speed of lightening! This, of course, will all happen with you now using only a mere 20 percent (more) effort in what you're already doing, before your dreams are tangibly manifested.

SO, DREAMERS, LET'S GET STARTED!

CHAPTER 3: THE FIRST KEY LAW: SEEK FIRST THE KINGDOM

Instructions from the Original Creator

Your dreams and desires are really the key origin of all things. They are indeed the wonderful origin and creator of all worthy desires and wishes you have or will ever manifest in your life. Yet, this key 20 percent area or thing in which all things are first created has to be isolated, identified, and sought first by simply connecting with another invisible key 20 percent area or thing in our lives that we all have accessible to us. Believe it or not, this other key thing we must first isolate, identify, and then "seek first" is actually our own "mind." This is the first key universal law, before creating any real dreams in life. There have been many business, self-help, spiritual, and personal development books written (many of which I have read) on how to achieve and reach dreams and goals in life. Yet, few have touched on the key spiritual and lawful order in which these dreams and goals must effortlessly come about, nor the key spiritual origin of, and behind, those dreams. This key information must also be isolated, identified, and known, and then incorporated in creating any lasting dream in our lives. Needless to say, I personally over time in my life have not found a self-help, spiritual, business, or personal development book that has touched on or explored this subject.

"The 80/20 spiritual method" which encompasses and shields light on "every" key (20 percent) thing invisibly nested (yet readily available) in our everyday life that will mysteriously create and thereafter multiply and turbo-boost into existence every single dream you have buried deep within you, all with little of your effort. Yes, those wonderful dreams we all have of good health, wonderful relationships with others in our lives, a beautiful soul mate relationship, a successful family life, a wonderful career, and financial abundance. These dreams, your key heart's desire, can all indeed become yours for the simple taking and acceptance when you know how to isolate and tap into those key mental, spiritual, and emotional key (20 percent) faculties invisibly nested in yourself, as you are now effortlessly doing by simply reading this book, this will ignite and thereafter effortlessly turbo-boost all those wonderful, fulfilling dreams, and needs you have in your life bringing them forth in a wonderful, lawful, and effortless manner.

YOUR NEEDS IN LIFE

You can indeed have those twanging dreams and goals, just mentioned above, manifest in your life now in an accelerated short-time period over your life. You can, believe it or not, have all those dreams happen in your life starting today, using less of your worries, time, money, energy, and other efforts. It's important to note here that aside from yours, and every other person's basic key needs in life of food, shelter, clothing, oxygen, and water, which are really just the 20 percent basic animal survival needs required by any lower animal species, all other key (80 percent) needs that we as "human animals" have are called, "spiritual needs." These key needs can only be met by the key and spiritual laws that govern the manifestation of those needs, which we all simply call, or refer to as, our "dreams and goals" in life.

Believe it or not, when you were created, you were indeed created with the innate, inborn ability, and beautiful key capacity to dream, the only key 20 percent vehicle that your creator (GOD) knew you needed to meet those spiritual needs we all have to keep us continuously inspire and journey through this thing called "Life," despite any of the obstacles and nightmares that would occur over time in our lives.

I am quite sure that you have heard it said on numerous occasions that a man or woman without a dream is "dead," which simply means they are breathing, yet they are dead mentally, spiritually, and emotionally. They are alive similar to a patient being supported on an artificial respirator, but all else is dead. The doctor has indeed pronounced him "humanly dead," without the beautiful and wonderful 80 percent spiritual and survival need, this wonderful innate ability to dream.

The dreams and goals you and I have for our life were in essence given to us. Those dreams and goals would have not been given to us if we weren't able and equipped to receive and thereafter carry them forth in an effortless manner. So in truth, our dreams, as well as our needs and our goals to accomplish those dreams in our lives are really our "Higher Power's" dreams, needs, and goals for us first. Yes, they are God's dreams and missions for our lives first simply revealed to us as our dreams and goals, to be individually expressed by us, not the reverse, which many may be led to believe. These dreams and goals may merely appears as one coming up with his own "fantastic fantasy" or mental image in their own mind first, and then asking or praying that their Higher Power or God confirms or affirms their fantasy dream for him. The dreams, which you may refer to as your "Goals" in your life, in fact, will be simply offered over intervals of time in your life, for your simple taking and thereafter effortless build up of firm faith and belief in those offered dreams. For this is the key "Law of Belief," and how this law really works. Not the other way, as mentioned above. So with this possible new enlightenment, you must know that your true dream(s) can only be spiritually or even psychologically enlightened to you via connecting with that source (or that spiritual mind) that is offering or giving you those dreams.

HOW YOUR DREAMS ARE CREATED

The method described in the following paragraphs believe, it or not, is the only key psychological or spiritual method in which those enlightened dreams or goals for your life will be offered, suggested, or effortlessly revealed to you, and thereafter effortlessly carried out for you. This is simply by, and through, your ongoing "silent individual prayer" (this key little effort) where you then ask for your dreams and goals in life. "Why prayer?" you may quickly ask. It's because this key word "prayer," according to *Webster's English Dictionary*, simply means your "earnest request." You're in essence "earnestly requesting" or "seeking" your dreams or goals by connection through prayer with that source, which will then give you your dreams and your goals for your life. This key source you're connecting with is "your higher power" (God). This is what's called connecting with, or "seeking the kingdom," a little key (20 percent) action you must perform by entering and connecting with your own individual "mind," called "The Kingdom" to ask for your dreams already commissioned, by "God's mind," your higher power especially for you.

Once this is done, there is really little effort for you to then perform. Aside from waiting, a little key (20 percent) more effort (of using time) you must perform. Your dream, without fail, over a short interval of time will be, thereafter, mysteriously revealed to you. Believe it or not, it will later be revealed to you again through that same channel, which is through your own individual "mind." It will be silently revealed and shown to you by an unconscious and inaccessible instinctual (20 percent) part of your brain, defended in many medical or standard dictionaries as the "id" part of your personality, this mysterious part of your mind which is part of your distinct "psyche" or "personality" that was given to you when you were created. This "id" part of your mind is for the sole purpose of seeking expression of an "ideal." This little key invisible and mysterious part of your mind will then mysteriously, thereafter, cause you to form a mental vision, or imaged dream, of something in your mind, simply called an "idea." This idea or vision formed in your mind is the vision and idea of your dream or goal that you have sought, requested, and awaited from "The Kingdom" (your mind) being revealed (or simply suggested) to you.

This is the only key spiritual and psychological method and origin in which all real dreams are enlightened to us in life. This has been the logic behind why I have named this book *Dream It First.*

Once an idea or vision of your dream or goal is perceived and shown, as illustrated above, there is very little effort for you to do thereafter, aside from you simply mentally accepting and affirming that dream or goal in your life with firm faith, belief, and conviction, which I will show you how to do. For the dream envisioned to you is indeed yours, regardless of the invisible, psychological, and unconscious spiritual faculties used to bring it about, as just illustrated above. This implies that there's really little physical effort for you to do. No (100 percent) forcing needed on your part, as shown in Chapter 2. There is no need for reservations on your part, your need for any continued prayer to request for that same dream, or another dream or goal in place of that one. Although it may be difficult for you to initially believe the dream or goal shown to you, regardless of its size, nature, contents, or whatever else is happening simultaneously in your life, it's definitely yours. This "dream" is now ready to be expressed to the world by you. Spiritual law, thereafter, will effortlessly go to work in gradually attracting, aligning, and realigning all the things and events in your life for the proper "how and when" of that dream's occurrence, and the physical manifestations of that dream. This will be that "Law of Attraction," about which you may have recently heard many speak and write. This attraction is "Your Higher Power's mind," which many will only refer to as "God" going to work on your behalf attracting your dreams to you. This will happen, of course, only after your full mental "acceptance and belief" in that dream that's been perceived or shown to you. Then and only then will the mysterious 80 percent work on "how and when" those dreams will be manifested shall go into play, as previously shown to you in Chapter 2. Again, there will be little for you to do aside from you, of course, "Thankin' God (your Higher Power)" for that dream. This acknowledgment is the same acknowledgment you would give to anyone in return for anything you have accepted from them. After this is done, the only key thing you must do thereafter over time is to begin to build an ongoing affirming faith, belief, and conviction in that dream revealed to you in your own mind first. This can easily, without much effort, be accomplished simply by you following and acknowledging the laws being outlined and presented to you in this book you now hold.

SO, DREAMERS, LET'S GET STARTED!

Yes! The true dreams you have for yourself were in essence derived from this place call "The Kingdom," as shown above, and they will again be expressed through that same "Kingdom" your own "mind." Yes, they will then be expressed through and by your own ongoing positive "thoughts" about those dreams enlightened to you, those thoughts you loudly express to yourself and to others in the world. All this will stem from your "mind." This is the reasoning for the complex statement you may have heard that "Mind is everything," which sounds so confusing to many. Why? Because those thoughts produced from your mind over time will guide the directions of any dreams and goals in your life. It is interesting to note here that the word "thought," as defined in many American dictionaries, simply as our "process of thinking." This "process of thinking" is what we all refer to as our "thoughts." These thoughts, thereafter, over time will mysteriously lead our emotions, and finally our actions in life. This is what will lead to manifesting or deterring the manifestation of our dreams in life, all depending on how our "thinking process," or how our thoughts are used. If your thinking process, or thoughts, is interrupted, they then will over time not be free to flow, and will cause interruptions or separation from your focus on your enlightened dreams given to you. This will happen without fail, when we have allowed two key negative things to occur: One, not mentally accepting your dreams given to you with firm faith and belief after they have been revealed to you, because of your fear, as to how and when those dreams will be manifested over time. And two, getting too distracted for too long of a period by the present or past "nightmares" that have occurred in your life.

These two key things will, in fact, distract your thinking process or your thoughts, and will over time take your thoughts and focus away from your enlightened dreams. Your thinking on these negative things will over time lead to your negative emotions or feelings, and finally your negative actions in life pertaining to your dreams, because your positive thoughts about your enlightened dream have then been replaced. They have been replaced with negative and self-limiting thoughts pertaining to the nightmares you may be currently experiencing, or a combination of other negative, distracting thoughts. Yes, again, those thoughts of "how and when" those enlightened dreams will come into play or existence for you.

LACK AND LIMITATION

The above type of mental thinking in essence is called "Mental Lack and Limitation," in your own mind a big 80 percent effect or negative result in our thinking mentality about our dreams after they have been enlightened to us, which will surely only provides us with approximately 20 percent, or even less, of what we really want in life.

This "Lack and Limitation" mentality may imply to you in your thinking that you are indeed "limited" in your ability to attain those key dreams, simply because of the unknown factors of "how and when" those enlightened dreams will be physically manifested over time. This type of thinking mentality will surely prevent your dreams from ever manifesting. This, and your full concentration and focus given to any of your current or past nightmares in your life, will surely over time take all your dreams away. All those unsound false beliefs that actually incant "No!" to you about those dreams enlightened to you are definitely untrue. Believe me when

I say this: any and all types of negative thinking in your mind in relationship to or towards your enlightened dreams in life are definitely unsound and false. Why? Because your dreams have been given to you, and they have been custom ordered. This denotes that they will be automatically carried out on your behalf for you every single time, regardless of any of the unknown factors you do not have. This will happen regardless of whatever else is happening in your life. This type of "Lack and Limitation" mental thinking will always over time imply to you in your thinking in reference to your dreams that there is something called "Lack" (a shortage of something, or not enough of something) that is, a lack, or shortage of time, money, energy, knowledge, or other resources which again is definitely untrue. Since your dream was dreamt for you, how can there possibly be anything lacking to bring about its physical manifestation? This "Lack and Limitation" (mentality and thinking), which often manifests in many people's thinking once a dream has been enlightened or offered to them, is what also causes them to have "fear" and "anxiety" in their lives about their dreams. This anxiety that they may be experiencing is really the fear of the unknown about how and when those dreams enlightened to them will, in fact, be physically manifested. This, as shown earlier, shouldn't really be of concern to them.

Fear and anxiety that many harbor in their lives will not allow them to have their enlightened dreams, causing them, even without their full awareness, to harbor resentment and even envy towards those who have effortlessly accepted their dreams in their lives. What they may not know is that a little key element called "spiritual law" has done the 80 percent work for those who have (over time) simply "accepted" their dreams. Dreams that others may view from afar yet do not often understand how they have occurred.

This is why many self-development books, as well as many great philosophies, incant throughout their contents the following message: "Do not be afraid." The bible also incants throughout its contents "Fear ye not," "I have not given you the spirit of fear," and "Do not be anxious for anything." Why are these anti-fear and anti-anxiety statements incanted? Because "fear" and "anxiety" (these two ugly 80% elements) are the big 80 percent or more deadly element and killer of all dreams enlightened to us. So, in essence, our letting go of this 80 percent "fear factor" and immediately replacing it with the beautiful 20 percent "factor of faith" must be the little 20 percent more effort that we must perform over time. This increased faith we must have is simply having a greater belief and conviction in your dreams given to you. This step of "faith" has to be the "next key step" that surely must occur after anyone has been given a recognition or enlightenment of any dreams in their lives.

LETTING GO AND LETTING FAITH

This next key step, as mentioned above, of "letting go" of fear means not looking at the physical effects. All 80 percent of nightmares, and all the other things, that say "No" to you about your enlighten dreams, or the so-called "how and the when" those dreams are to come about. These apparent "facts" you do not have, as to the methods to be used in bringing forth those enlightened dreams into existence in your life. This should not be of concern to you. You must simply mentally, as well as physically, if you need to, "turn away, and do not allow these things to move you," as quoted in the Bible. You should not feed mentally, physically, or emotionally into these ostensible facts that appear real, yet are not! Do not become sidetracked by their appearances, which may be surrounding your dreams, telling you "No" to, or about, anything pertaining to your enlightened dreams given to you.

Such things that others in authority over you, those close to you, or even you yourself, may say that's negative about your enlightened dream can include, "You don't have the money," "You don't know the right people," "You can't," "You're not situated yet," "How can you?" "You just lost your job," "You're too old," "You don't have the time," "You don't know how it's going to work out," "You just went through a divorce," "What if this or that happens?" and so on. Those are among the other negative objections and walls that may be put up by others, as well as yourself. These counters are all just ostensible walls that are put up every time a dream has been enlightened to you to simply deter you, if you allow them to do so, from you manifesting your dreams in life, although these counters heard from you, as well as others in your life, may be what we all may refer to as "100 percent factual information" and "facts" that may support this factual information given. You must know and discern here, as will be unfolded to you throughout in this book, that there's no truth behind those 100 percent ostensible facts.

There have been many self-developments books written on how to achieve goals and dreams in one's life. Yet they all incant basely the same little 20 percent message the Bible incants: "Judge not according to the appearances of things," which basically means do not judge, concentrate, or focus on the negative 100 percent about your dreams given to you, but judge only by a 20 percent effort called "faith" and belief. We are, indeed, instructed to have faith, giving only our full focus, concentration, and attention to our dreams in life. We are instructed to only give our full judgment of things that are positive pertaining to our enlightened dreams in life. You should not give away any of your focus or any of your attention or your emotions to any of the negative appearances and things surrounding those dreams, because they will only provide you with approximately 20 percent, or even less, of what you truly want in life, if they are focused on or given your full 80 percent or more attention.

We all, including myself, may sometimes get off-track over time, having the tendency to feed into the negative "facts," all the 100 percent negatives about our dreams, and all the nightmares occurring in our life that surround our enlightened dreams. Yet, when our dreams in our lives (this little 20 percent key) are unleashed, we begin to build a mental, spiritual, and emotional equal of those desired dreams in our lives, first in our minds, before they're physically manifested. The "facts and all the nightmares pertaining to how and when those enlightened dreams will be manifested will be of little importance. All the stuff we all hear, such as "How will I make it happen?" "I don't have the money," "I'm too old," and so on, will no longer be of concern to you. You will see this, just by you now focusing only with a mere 20 percent more effort on the positive aspects of your dream, with your mind, body, and spirit, which is what we will cover in the following chapter. This will be all that is important in manifesting your dreams. This is the only effort that will be needed to begin physically manifesting every enlightened dream you have for yourself.

Not having or seeing in your immediate possession your 80 percent, or all the things and all the means you may think are necessary to create those dreams in your life, is none of your concern or business. It may be very hard to understand the following statement: "It was never really any of your business or concern." Only 20 percent of what is accessible to you, which are your higher powers, as shown earlier, is your only concern, and what's needed to provide you the 80 percent means of how and when your dreams will be manifested for you. With this in mind, you in essence truly have to start learning how to "let go" of your own conscious control, and your own "know-how," and learn to "Lean not to your own understanding of things," as quoted in the Bible. Let go of the 100 percent, and let your 20 percent do the work to take you to your 80 percent, or more, in your life.

Let go of your old thinking and your old (non-effective) 100 percent effort ways of doing things, and be renewed or transformed by a 20 percent more effort called "the renewing of your mind." Let go of your own "control" and perform this little 20 percent more effort of allowing spiritual law, which governs all dreams, to pioneer and create those dreams for you. This is the only natural thing for you to now do in your life. "Letting go" is simply replacing our own old control and fear of things with a little 20 percent more effort called "faith," which is having a powerful belief and conviction in your dreams. This is the only little thing you will need to do in your life, prior to you demonstrating your dreams in life, as will be shown to you in Chapter 5. Yet, what is this little key 20 percent effort that we now know of called "faith"? It is indeed a law within itself, for "faith," as defined in the bible, is simply "The substance of things hoped for, and the evidence of things not seen." This, again, is the 'Law of Faith and Belief" without any form of doubt. As you may not have seen, the tangible means it is more important for you to first build up your other 20 percent faculties, which are your mental, spiritual, and emotional faculties. This, thereafter, will produce a spiritual equivalent for your physical dream, not yet physically seen. This must be done in your mind first, before your dreams will thereafter tangibly manifest in your life for you.

WHO ARE YOU?

Without your awareness, you are, believe it or not, an individual expression of "God," made in God's image, and likeness by God, according to Genesis 1: 26-27. This means that when you were created by God, you were created in his same likeness and image with Him giving you the same mind qualities He possesses. The only difference you have your own dominion and "free will" over your mind given to you. So it must also hold true that your mind and God's mind are, in actuality, the same mind, with the only difference being that you are free to use your own mind any way you choose for positive or negative effects you may or may not obtain by the use of that given "free will" of your mind. Although this may sound somewhat foreign to many, it's factually sound and true. What you should now know with this possible new defining truth is that when you first seek God, "The Kingdom," as shown earlier, you're actually seeking yourself, or foremost, to first know yourself. This small 20 percent more effort that you must take is what will take you to your greater 80 percent or more results and those enlightened dreams in your life. If you choose to reword this statement, or even approach it in a totally different manner and only seek yourself first, with this little 20 percent more effort, you are in essence first "seeking to know God." This small 20 percent more effort is what's also needed to take you to your greater 80 percent or more in your life. Either way you choose to approach or word these actions, you are actually seeking what's called "The Kingdom," that sacred "Higher Power" or "Higher Self." Either way, you are seeking that quiet and sacred place within your mind, that key (20 percent) place to simply let go and release the conscious and physical outer world, and to accept your dreams and missions for your life. This will, ultimately, manifest what we refer to as our dreams and goals in every area of our lives every single time, without fail.

In this key 20 percent place, which we now know is called "The Kingdom," we release the outer stuff from the entire outer world, all the "No's" we and others in the world may say or impose to us about our dreams. We slowly move all of this stuff out of the way, and we get in touch with our "Higher Self," that "Higher Power," that "mind" and image that God has made in his own likeness, which is YOU.

YOUR FINAL ACCEPTANCE

Once the vision of your dream has been given to you, as shown earlier, it's imperative that you then mentally "accept" and "believe" that dream is yours. Although your dream may not be physically there yet, it's of great importance that you mentally perform the small 20 percent action of "accepting" that dream. You mentally believe the visional dream revealed to you is yours without any form of conscious doubt, as this step is "your key 20 percent" a very important one that must be turned before your dreams can begin to effortlessly manifest and come into full existence in your life. This is literally true with anything one mentally, as well as physically, accepts in their life that's been given to them, whether the thing that's given to them is positive or negative. I recall the time my son, Raymond, was nearly fatally wounded in the head when he was eighteen years old. After being taken off of life support, he began his long and gruesome physical rehabilitation program. Months afterwards, the head physician over the rehabilitation department at the hospital reluctantly informed us he had appeared to have hit a "plateau," that his rehabilitation and therapy program was over, and we needed to be prepared for him never to walk again without some form of outside assistance. His cerebellum, located at the base of his brain that controlled his balance, had been gravely damaged by the near-fatal gunshot wound he had encountered to his head. To the doctor's surprise, as the doctor later revealed to me, he candidly told her in a private conversation which they had together, "That's not true at all! My mother has told me that she has worked with patients in Occupational Therapy much worse than me, and that I will walk again. So, doctor, I'm really not worried about that." Why was my son able to counter this doctor's poor medical prognosis of never being able to freely walk again? Because he had "turned" the only key he had available to him. He had simply already mentally accepted his dream (given to him) of being able to walk freely, with unshakable mental belief and conviction. He wasn't about to allow this very confident doctor, or her skilled therapy team, to take his enlightened dream away. The hospital and their rehabilitation therapy team, well, they did discharge my poor son home in a wheelchair with that unfortunate poor prognosis that they had all predicted, but the wheelchair they sent him home in was never used. If you were to see my son today, you would have never known this unfortunate story by simply looking at him, as he is quite well, and yes, walking quite independently! Yes, it is definitely true that if anyone just does the 20 percent more work required of simply turning on their key of "acceptance" and thereafter building an ongoing affirming mental belief, faith, and conviction in everything pertaining to that enlightened dream, regardless of any "poor prognosis given," this is the only real little 20 percent effort they will ever need to do until the time that dream is finally manifested. This is what I'll be showing you how to easily do in the following chapter. This will, without any doubt, be the only "little effort that will give you much" in your life, for it is definitely the little hidden key 20 percent effort that will, without fail, provide you your greater 80 percent and more results of what you're seeking in your life, every single time.

SO, DREAMERS, LET'S GET STARTED!

CHAPTER 4: THE LAW OF CREATION

Three Key Steps Used To
Create All Dreams

When the universe was first created, there were three steps that were used. These will be shown to you in this and the following chapter. God, the true creator of all our enlightened dreams in life, has concise instructions on how anyone's dreams in life are to be effortlessly created, once they have been enlightened to them (as shown in Chapter 3). Yet few, maybe only 20 percent, of our population, it seems, has been able to discern these orderly instructions, and as a result of this unknown and key information many have often foundered in (effortlessly) being able to manifest and turbo burst their enlightened dreams and goals in life.

Believe it or not, all dreams, including those enlightened to you, must also be molded after some of those same key "steps" used when God created the universe, that is, if you wish to have a near perfect (approximately 80 percent or more) manifestation or demonstration of any dream, as will be shown to you in this chapter, and in the following chapter entitled "In The Beginning."

All dreams ever dreamt or ever created by any person, whether they were aware of these steps or not, used these same 20 percent steps. Yes! Believe it or not, Jesus used these same key three steps for his accepted mission in life. Donald Trump used these steps. Mahatma Gandhi used these steps. So did Bill Gates, Barack Obama, Oprah Winfrey, Mother Teresa, and Martin Luther King Jr. (who in turn shared his enlightened dream to the world). All these great people and many other great dreamers we know of in life all used these same 20 percent effort steps when they created their enlightened dreams in their life. Again, whether they were aware of these orderly steps or not, they did in fact use them. I am sure that in many cases some of them may not have been consciously aware of these steps. Nevertheless, consciously or unconsciously, they used them prior to their dreams ever becoming a real physical manifestation in their lives.

One of the reasons you have possibly chosen this book is that you have a dream or goal in life, and you wish, apparently, to forego the "trial and error" 100 percent effort process. Therefore, you option for the wisdom of others (another 20 percent more effort) in lieu of the long "trial and error" process. But note here that regardless of either of the above methods you choose to use, in truth, you will eventually arrive at your dream(s), but with far less time, money, effort, and energy, as well as having and achieving your dream over time in a faster, orderly, and more permanent fashion, simply by learning from the experience and great wisdom of others. By following the steps that are now being unfolded to you here in this book, you'll be learning and receiving your wisdom, not only from me, but directly from the cosmic "great inventor and Creator" of all dreams, which is "God," your key 20 percent in everything.

SO, DREAMERS, LET'S BEGIN!

To aid you in understanding the following three key steps, prior to them being introduced to you, I would like for you to take a few moments and close your eyes, and remember (without forcing) back at a time in your life where there was something, either large or small, that you observed or recognized as an effortless manifestation of a dream in your life.

Maybe it was a toy that you dreamt of as a child. Maybe it was the dream of getting and maintaining straight As in school. Maybe it was the dream (or desire) to stop smoking or meeting your soul mate, that special someone in your life, or the dream of purchasing a desired home or car. Possibly the dream was starting a business.

Now without you being aware of it, some things were taking place over time prior to that dream ever becoming a physical realization in your life. What was happening is what I like to call the "20 percent preparation steps" or "prep steps" for that dream, or the preparing for that dream. Unbeknown to you, this 20 percent preparation was taking place mentally, meaning in your thinking, spiritually, meaning in your faith, and emotionally, meaning in your feelings, way before that actual dream ever manifested in your life.

Let's examine here what happened.

Step 1: First over time there was a thought, a, vision about that thing, that dream, which was the first creation step. You had to have had an idea first (as shown in Chapter 1) about that toy, about becoming a non-smoker, about that soul mate relationship, that car, that house, that business you started. These thoughts were a mental (visual) equivalent, or mental equal for that dream that you had desired, which had to occur first.

Step 2: There then over time was a firm "build up" of affirmed faith (or belief) in and about that thing or desired dream. There was a building of faith and belief in and about that toy, becoming a non-smoker, the soul mate relationship, the car, the house, the business. Now, although the evidence of that thing or dream was not physically there, you had already developed an unshakable affirmed and firm faith, an unshakable belief and conviction. You just knew that you knew that you knew! You were going to have that dream, and this was all you could think or talk about. This is what is called a spiritual equivalent, or equal for that thing or dream (over time), which was the second step that had to occur.

Step 3: Your emotions at that point over time had become so strong, so intense, about that desired dream, that you really felt like you already had it. You felt like that dream was already yours, although it was not physically there. This was an emotional equivalent for that dream, which was the third step that had to occur. You, in fact, had carried that "baby" long enough, and when it was ready to come, nothing could stop it. Note here that this preparation is similar to what a mother "in waiting" goes through over time as she awaits her newborn to come. She, in actuality, has prepared for this "manifestation" or "demonstration," i.e. the baby arriving.

She has prepared for the baby mentally (i.e. visualizing the baby's arrival), spiritually (having the faith, belief, and conviction in the baby arriving), emotionally (she felt like that the baby had already arrived, way before its physical manifestation).

These three steps were simply the 20 percent preparation for that dream. The 20 percent preparation was mentally, spiritually, and emotionally even before that dream manifested physically. For a mental, spiritual, and emotional equivalent or equal for that dream over time had occurred in your mind first prior to it ever arriving physically. Again, these were just the 20 percent prep steps for that dream, or any dream created, and accounts for the old saying that "All dreams are dreamt twice," meaning in your Mind first and then (second) over time in physical form.

Note here that although all three of these steps were over time occurring in a systematic, orderly (divine, spiritual, subconscious, automatic, and involuntarily) fashion, and you were building up an affirming mental, spiritual, and emotional equivalent or equal for that dream in a lawful orderly manner in your mind. What you did not know was the how and the when for that dream. What you did not know was how or when that dream was to actually come about. Although, you may have had inkling or a hypothesis about how it was going to happen, or approximately when it was going to happen, the truth was you really did not know at all.

On many occasions, I'm sure your dream didn't even occur the way, or even when, you thought it would have happened. This was because, at this point of you affirming and building a mental, spiritual, and emotional equivalent for that dream in your mind first, your job was finished and complete. You had already done the 20 percent preparation for that dream, which was all that was needed. You had already over time done the preparation mentally, spiritually, and emotionally, which was a 20 percent spiritual equal of that (physical) dream desired. This was the only 20 percent action required by you before that dream effortlessly physically manifested.

Thereafter, spiritual law this key 20 percent element went to work on providing the means for that dream to occur, which was the 80 percent of how and when that dream was to be manifested. One of the reasons many fail to have their true dreams manifest or endure at this point is because after they have performed the 20 percent effort steps, as indicated above, which is all that's really needed, or required, they then attempt to take on the control of forcing the how and when that dream will manifest. This 80 percent means, as mentioned in the previous pages, this was none of their concern or business. Yet, many put a 100 percent effort and force into working and taking on how and when the dream is to occur, when it was not needed at all. As we now know from chapter 2 of this book, approximately 80 percent or more of all results will flow or come from only 20 percent or less of their effort over time, not from the 80 percent or 100 percent effort. How and when the dream is manifested over time is the unknown factor. Nevertheless, we can always use the results of its manifestation in our lives. Allowing spiritual law over time to take care of the means as to how and when that dream will manifest is very, and I mean very, much of a challenge, believe it or not, for approximately 80 percent, or more of the population in the world. This may be why we only see what appears to be only 20 percent or less of the people in the world over time truly living their dreams. This also accounts for why we see what looks like, as we discussed in Chapter 1, only a few esoteric, or "lucky" 20 percent, groups of people in the world manifesting their true dreams, while others appear to founder in the manifestations of their dreams in life, where in essence what has occurred is that they simply over time use the laws. That is, "The 80/20 Law" coupled with this beautiful "Law of Creation," these two "key 20 percent elements" available to them, as well as to you.

HAPPINESS
How it is Created Using the "20 Percent Prep Steps"

Before we leave this chapter, "The Law of Creation," in which we now know and see how all dreams are molded, I would like to show here, how "happiness" or the "state of happiness," this key intangible dream we all have, is also created and molded using the same 20 percent effort shown to you earlier.

As I speak to numerous audiences on the subject of obtaining happiness and success in life, what I have discerned, which has been my motivation for such public talks, is that everyone is in pursuit of this dream called happiness. Many will go through extreme (100 percent) efforts in their lives just to obtain this happiness, a word which we will see in the following sentence is just a mere "spiritual state." If looked up in any dictionary, the word "happiness" is simply defined as "being in a mental & spiritual state." This is what this so-called "happiness" really is, and this is what truly produces the "happiness" we're all in search of. This further explains why we are all merely in search of the same thing, "meeting a spiritual need," this key spiritual need and drive that we simply call "happiness" in our lives. This key need or drive we all have is not a material or physical need or drive, which most may think they're in search of. It is a spiritual need that we are in search of. This also further explains our 80 percent human "spiritual needs," as described earlier in Chapter 3. With this in mind one must know, and may more easily understand, why happiness cannot, or is not derived over time, from the 80 percent or more outer physical and material things in the world. Why? Because it is not a physical need we are in search of, but a "spiritual need," which cannot be obtained or met by the simple accumulation of material possessions and money. How can it be? If it is, as we now know, a "mental and spiritual" need (as described above), this may account for why so many people in the world who do possess huge amounts of money or many physical possessions are not always "happy" or in a positive mental and spiritual state, although they possess all those things the masses in the world think would or should make them happy. Have you ever pondered this question? If you have, the following may explain to you the answer.

Simply because (as described above) this thing called "happiness" that we want in life is not derived from the external, but from within that 20 percent spiritual place that we all have within us. You may hear many people make the statements that they will only be happy when a certain event (outside of themselves) occurs in their life. "I'll be happy when I get married, purchase a home, purchase a car, raise my children, get out of this bad marriage, painstaking job, or get out of prison." They may even believe that when they become a millionaire, or when they win the lottery is when they will become "happy," yet what happens when some or even all of these things occur? They get married, win the lottery, purchase the home of their dreams, their children grow up and leave home. They get out of a bad marriage or job, or even out of jail. What happens when all the other things they thought would make them "happy" does occur? Yes, they may obtain that "mental and spiritual" state or that so-called "happiness," but this type of "happiness," or "mental and spiritual state" cannot last or endure simply because their happiness they're in search of is solely based on external events outside of themselves, occurring first in their lives. If one has not first built a "mental and spiritual state," this 20 percent effort over time in their lives first, one simply becomes a "Dream Chaser," also called a "Wanter" in life (which we will cover in the following chapter), simply chasing and wanting dream after dream, in their search of that permanent "mental and spiritual state" called "happiness," yet only getting that temporary "high," or spiritual rush before they're out chasing, wanting, or looking for another dream in their lives.

This is really an "addiction," a real "bad habit!" If one has not used the 20 percent prep steps over time before their outer material 80 percent is added to them, they, in fact, will not be happy once they do obtain those things. Yes, that same mental, spiritual, and emotional equivalent for that "happiness" has to be created over time first. This is with everything in life that is created. It must over time be built and created in one's own mind first. A spiritual equal for their dreams of happiness has to over time be built first in their own mind, regardless of any of their current circumstances in life, before their dream of happiness is manifested. If not, they will not be happy when the outer physical things they desire do occur over the time in their lives. What this means is one has to be happy in their lives right now with whatever it is they are presently doing or have, or do not have now, in their lives. This also equates to them being graceful for what they do have, not only waiting for the day when those things on the outside (of them) happens. If they do not do this, they will not be able to obtain that permanent "mental or spiritual" state, which we now know is called "happiness" in their lives when those things on the outside of them does occur in their lives. When one's "happiness" is created and built according to this "Law of Creation," shown here in this chapter, their happiness is something that no event, person, or thing over time can ever take away from them, which accounts for the old cliché that "Nothing can ever (permanently) take your happiness away unless you choose to allow it." This may also account for the little tune the whole world fell in love with in the '90s called "Don't Worry, Be Happy." So it must also follow that if one wants "happiness," they must simply perform the same 20 percent preparation steps of building a mental, spiritual, and emotions equal over time for that same "happiness" in their own mind and their present life first, before their happiness can be permanently given when their outer dreams and desires do occur in their lives. When it's all built mentally and spiritually (first), and last emotionally, it is in this final accumulated (Mental and Spiritual) state that the "Dry Land" has said to have appeared, for in this final state is the dream they have always been seeking their in life.

CHAPTER 5: IN THE BEGINNING

As we have now seen in the preceding chapter "The Law of Creation," all dreams ever dreamt in life were in fact over time modeled after this same beautiful law that governs the manifestation of all dreams in anyone's life. It may only make logical sense to examine here in this chapter a succinct synopsis of the creation process used when the universe itself was first created. This is the reasoning behind this chapter being titled "In the Beginning," to depict what this "Law of Creation" implies from a biblical perspective, and what it may also possibly imply to you, as you, too, now begin to create your dreams and goals in life, modeled and crafted after this beautiful law of creation we have just covered.

SO, DREAMERS, LET'S BEGIN!

When the universe was originally created over time by the great creator of all things, "God," there were three steps also included, which are in essence the same three steps just shown to you in the previous chapter. As previously noted in the last chapter with all dreams created, there must first be "an enlightenment." This is followed simply with a strong "building" of affirming "faith, belief, and conviction" in everything pertaining to that dream. This building of faith, belief, and convictions has to be developed over time in your mind, mentally, spiritually, and finally emotionally first, as shown in Chapter 3, before that dream is physically manifested. This accounts for why so many people's dreams are not always fully physically manifested, because they're often just quickly building their dreams only emotionally first. This accounts for the frustration many may feel after a failed, short-term relationship, or after leaving a motivational talk or a Sunday church service. They may have initially felt empowered emotionally, yet they are still unable to thereafter carry forth a full physical manifestation of their dreams in their lives. Why? Because it was built quickly and only emotionally first, which will not last or endure. All three of these steps must be built over time, and are needed, and these three steps cannot be skipped. These are the only three steps needed! They must be included over time for any real dream to manifest. It will take time before those dreams are fully built. Those dreams will manifest, but the precise method of manifestation is the only unknown factor in the dream creation process. This is the reason why most people feel the urgent need, at this point of the process, to "force" the physical manifestation with their own "know how," self-control, and excessive 100 percent effort called "force," which we now know provides less in contrast to more of their desired dream. In fact, the only thing one does have full control over, and can effortlessly perform to decrease the time it will actually take to build and manifest those enlightened dreams, is to simply perform just a mere 20 percent more effort of whatever they may be currently doing, to build up a greater mental level of belief and faith in that enlightened dream. They must do this over time mentally, spiritually, and finally emotionally. This is really all one can, or needs to do, to facilitate and quicken the "dream manifestation process" and physical presentation of their dreams in their life. This is the reason why we see so many successful and happy accomplished people, in all walks of life, as will be shown throughout this book, exerting little effort or force, being happy with whatever they do have in life, happily spending only approximately 20 percent or less of their time, money, and energy, and other resources, performing effortlessly the following things: Taking the time to build relationship with significant others in their lives, daily connecting with spirit via mediating, praying, reciting personal affirmation to themselves, performing mental visualizing of their dream(s), physically behaving and acting as though their desired dreams are already present in life, posting pictures of their dreams, giving themselves "positive self-talk," sharing their resources with others, and filling their minds daily with positive information by way of reading, attending spiritual and mental growth, and enrichment events, and maintaining a positive, upbeat, focused attitude in life, despite any of their apparent nightmares and occurrences in their lives. Why are they performing any one, or all, of these things? Simply because they are doing whatever it takes, within their own power, and personal preference (free will) to build and maintain their enlightened dreams with firm faith, belief, and conviction, prior to those dreams physically manifesting in their lives. They know that these things are the only (20 percent) efforts needed to be performed on their behalf, before spiritual law begins to go to work on their behalf in effortlessly manifesting their goals and dreams in life for them.

THREE STEPS OF CREATION

As shown earlier, all enlightened dreams in life must first go through two preparations steps, prior to the third step of your dream ever physically manifesting. These two preparation steps are:

1. Having an enlightenment of a dream.
2. Building a mental, spiritual, and emotional belief and faith in that enlightened dream, before the third step of one's dreams can physically occur or manifest in their lives.

This law is "The Law of Belief" that governs the creations or manifestations of all dreams ever created. This law actually stems, believe it or not, from three of the same steps used when "God" first created the universe. If anyone is familiar with Genesis, the first book of the Bible, we know that this is where it describes step-by-step how God over time first created "His dream" of the universe. Below is a succinct synopsis of three occurrences that did happen when the dream of the universe was initially formed and created, as illustrated in Genesis 1.

A SYNOPSIS OF THE THREE STEPS USED
Step 1: "A light." Genesis: 1:3
Step 2: "A firmament." Genesis: 1:6
Step 3: "The dry land appearing." Genesis: 1:9

The mental interpretation and definition of the above steps, as it pertains to creating our dreams in life, is as follows:

"Let there be light," as quoted in Genesis: 1:3, is saying (first) let there be an "enlightenment" or light of a dream.

"Let there be a firmament," as quoted in Genesis; 1:6, is saying (second) there must be a firmament or "making firm," of the building of firm belief and faith in that (enlightened) dream.

"Let the dry land appear," as quoted in Genesis: 1:9, is saying (third) the Dream must appear after it is built, and "made firm."

What the above is implying is that first there must always be a "light" or enlightenment of a dream. Second, there must always be a "firmament," or making firm, with the building of faith and belief in that enlighten dream. These two steps must occur over time prior to the third step of the dream physically becoming "dry land," or tangibly manifesting. Note here, again, that steps 1 and 2 above are simply the preparation steps for step 3, when the dream becomes "dry land," or is finally manifested.

These steps just shown to you are the 20 percent prep steps, or preparations steps, used before yours and anyone's dream will manifest. This is what some may refer to as a dream "coming to pass." It is, in fact, the only 20 percent effort you will ever need to do to provide you with approximately 80 percent (or more) of what you are looking for or ever dreamt in life. This statement is a very strong one. Why? Because if you have or will ever create any dreams in life that are intended for quality, quantity, and duration (meaning good), these three steps must be followed. They cannot be skipped.

This may account for why so many people in life have what I like to refer to as simply "wants," which never really manifest or become "dry land." Although they may mislabel these things as "dreams," they are in actuality not dreams at all, just simply "wants." These people have failed to use the two 20 percent "preparation steps" over time, as shown above, before their dreams become "dry land."

It is important to note here, again, that if one is not willing to forego this 20 percent more effort of doing the preparation steps, their dreams never really become a real manifestation in their life. They go through life continually attempting to have a demonstration or manifestation of their dreams in life without the "preparation," simply because they have failed to implement steps 1 and 2 of the dream manifestation process, essential in the creation process. However, you, a reader of this book, are not a mere "wanter," but a "real effortless dreamer." You have chosen to separate yourself from the "wanters" and "non-dreamers in life."

You are being equipped with clear, understandable knowledge on how this Law of Creation will work in your life to manifest every dream for you in life. You are now prepared to start living your dreams developed in an effortless, lawful order and fashion.

This law of creation and manifestation of your dreams will work over time in every single area of one's life without fail, believe it or not, for whatever dreams you hold. This is whether it's a long-term dream, or day-to-day dream. What I have discovered and discerned over time in my vast business and medical interaction with people in all walks of life, ranging from rich to poor, black to white, able-bodied to disabled, is that most people's apparent, often urgent needs, after their basic 20 percent survival needs are met in life, are that of having economic soundness, good health, and having and building good interpersonal relationships with the opposite gender as their number one objectives or dreams in life.

With a clear understanding of this law and how it works, regardless of the case or form, one can indeed have those immediate dreams, as well as their long-term needs and objectives become a physical realization and manifestation in their life. Starting today, whether it's the dream of having good health, getting out of debt, finding a soul mate, starting or building your own business, purchasing a material item, whatever that dream may be, when the 20 percent preparation steps for that dream are implemented prior to the demonstration, as previously shown, you can indeed have your true heart's desire.

LET'S EXAMINE HOW

We live in a very emotional and inpatient "time conscious" society, where everything we desire or want in life is "wanted yesterday." That's just how quickly we want our desires and our dreams in life, what those in the mental health field refer to as wanting "immediate gratification." This really denotes that the larger of our population (approximately 80 percent or more) has little time, desire, or ostensible need for any type of waiting or preparation for anything in life! Yet, many desperately want and will put 100 percent of their time, money, attention, energy, and effort into seeking to achieve an "immediate gratification" or demonstration of their dreams in life. This is contrary to this "Law of Creation," as has been shown to you thus far in this book. As we now see, that preparation (building faith and belief) does encompass some amount of time, and must be used, as this is the invisible 20 percent key that allows us 80 percent or more results in what we're seeking in life. This is the reason why most fail in their quests of their dreams ever becoming a near-perfect demonstration, as they fail to use the needed preparation (time) required in the preparation of their dreams. Yet, there does appear to be approximately 20 percent in the world's population who are using this law, and, yes, getting approximately 80 percent or more of what they truly desire of their dreams in their life. They have spent the needed small 20 percent more effort of time to "prepare" over time for the demonstration of their dreams.

Let's take a look at what I like to refer to as the emotional and inpatient "credit card trap," or our "high-speed emotional credit card society," and why so many people are literally emotionally and financially strapped on their paths to their dreams in life. A credit card simply provides a means or a form of emotional and financial "immediate gratification," without any real preparation (time). You simply fill out a bunch of applications, and in some cases just sign your name, and presto! You have that desired thing or that ostensible dream, or what appears to be a real dream, all which required no real preparation or time, as there was no time spent "building" anything! In fact, there was no preparation at all; no "steps one or two" were involved.

Just a speedy step number 3. or what appears to be a dream, simply because it looks very well like a real dream. The clothes, the cars, the trips, the house, and sometimes, even the relationships. They all just simply manifested out of the blue without any preparation, no steps 1 and 2 (enlightenment and build up). Now, the outside society, their friends, family, neighbors, co-workers, business associates, even themselves, are all fooled into thinking that they have had a "demonstration," a real dream to manifest in their lives.

Now, they are trapped into maintaining this façade of what looks like a successful dream just to keep up with the other 80 percent in the world that's doing the same thing, while they all suffer idly in silent mental, emotional and financial debt, this mental, spiritual emotional and financial pain. This is the real definition of the term "Mental Lack and Limitation," which I spoke of in Chapter 3, happening in their lives.

The reason why many suffer in silence, yet they look so good to the outside world, is because with their "dream look-a-like," the cars, the houses, the trips, the clothes, the relationships, they did not go through the creation steps or process, as shown to you earlier. There was no real preparation, no steps 1 and 2, prior to the demonstration of their "so-called dream." You see, when one's dreams are created, via these three steps shown to you earlier, there's never truly any suffering in maintaining their dreams. What others see is the "real thing," or a real dream, is a dream which never fails. They will then be free to go on in their lives, building dream after dream, never having to worry about losing those "real" dreams already built, unless they choose to let a dream of a lower level go. When they do appear to those in the 80 percent group in the world, to have let go of a dream, what they have really done is simply "let go" of something smaller, or an old dream to make room for a larger enlightened dream and goal that better serves their journey in life. These 20 percent dreamers can never really stop "dreaming," accepting, and building their enlightened dreams in their lives.

The lack of preparation, which equates to lack of time vested, is seen and felt in many personal relationships, as well as in one's quest for a real "soul mate." We, again, fail to go through the preparation steps, before we obtain a real dream relationship with another person in our lives.

Steps 1 and 2 of the preparation steps must still occur prior to the demonstration of a good relationship. Many relationships that are intended for marriage have simply failed in completing Steps 1 and 2. Their marriage was just put together in emotional haste for a "failed" demonstration, or what appears to be an ostensible dream, yet is not.

Let's look at what happens. As we recall in step 1 in the creation process, it does entail an "enlightenment" of something first, meaning an unfolding, discovery, discernment, recognition, or revelation of something. In this case, it is the revelation of a potential mate's assets, qualities, virtue, character, and personality. This needs to be discerned first, as shown earlier in Chapter 3 with the case of Mary. This does, in fact, take some amount of preparation and time before these things will manifest, or be enlightened, to anyone. Yet, as also mentioned earlier, we live in a very emotional, fast-paced society with little desire and time for any preparation for anything. This often results in a timeless, quick, and "failed" ostensible dream, or what appears to be a failed step 3 and demonstration. I currently own and operate a Legal Document/Paralegal business, which is part of our Real Estate firm. This division is supported mainly by my office assisting persons, who are in "pro per" (self attorney or self representing), with their legal documents for "Dissolution of Marriage." Many of our clients have related time after time that they only built their relationships emotionally and physically first and did not take the needed time to prepare, observe, and build their relationships mentally, spiritually or emotionally prior to getting married, which is what they now reluctantly relate as to what contributed to their apparent failed marriage. This I, too, can personally attest to as being the cause of my own short, failed marriage. My unfortunate experience in my divorce has been my core motivation for our office helping others, who are going through this often expensive and long legal process. We help them to leverage more of their time, money, and energy, as well as their emotional pain while going through this painstaking process. I, unfortunately, did not have the luxury of this assistance. Five judges, three money-oriented attorneys, and chronic six-year divorce, all amounted to fees of well over $49,000 in attorney costs alone. By our firm preparing the legal documents on the client's behalf, they can easily represent themselves through this often painful process by them simply leveraging more of their time, as well as their money, which many do not have in today's doubtful economy. What I have personally and painstaking learned by my own unfortunate experience is that you will always emotionally date what "appears" to be in a person, but you will always marry that real person. Adequate time spent with a potential soul mate in or before a marriage will surely manifest that real person's true mental, spiritual and emotional character and virtues, exposing who they really are to you every single time without fail. If you just take the time to simply identify those little key 20 percent areas, as Mary did in chapter 2, you will be able to easily assess what key areas or things are actually giving you less of what you want and more of what you do not want. I strongly suggest spending this time to identify and assess these key things before the marriage. It can definitely save you "way more with less" money, time, and emotional pain!

All this denotes that after the first step is completed in the dream process, and you have been given "enlightenment" or an unfolding of your potential mate's true character, virtue, as well as their personality, the second step in the creation process will begin. This will mainly consist of you building a faith and belief in what has been "enlightened" to you in that person, which again is their mental, spiritual and emotional character, virtue, and personality. This again can only be discerned by you spending quality time with the other person, via friendship-building, and happily bonding with that other person emotionally and intellectually, as shown earlier. This is what is meant by similarities blending and opposites attracting, for a real intended "soul mate."

This is what most relationship experts speak about. This is where one's weaknesses are seen as, or discerned as, the other person's strengths, and the other person's strengths are discerned as the other person's weakness. Opposites do attract as well as similarities, and with interests being of the same, they do blend. This is where one adds to, or completes and compliments, the other person mentally, spiritually and emotionally. This is the real beauty of a beautiful and true relationship, two people that are both whole (mentally, spiritually, and emotionally) coming together and becoming another "whole" person. This is why you hear the analogy that one and one is not two, but one and one together will equal three $(1+1=3)$. Two whole persons coming together spiritually in this manner produces a third whole person mentally, spiritually, and emotionally. What they mean are that those two whole minds coming together over time produces a third whole mind. What two persons can accomplish together over time is equal to there being a third whole person or third mind. These steps are truly essential prior to any permanent, long-term, good, quality, and quantitative relationship or dream, and it's one that can be definitely termed as a good demonstration and beautiful dream coming into manifestation. Yet, as mentioned earlier, in our emotional fast-paced society in which we live, everyone seemingly wants "immediate gratification," and as a result of this, we don't always prepare by using this little key 20 percent factor call "time" over the time in our lives.

That's the reason why we do not achieve what we want in life, which are our dreams. I have been in business for over half of my life, and I have heard and have applied (before my discovery of these spiritual laws being unfolded here in this book) many business theories. Most of you, who are in commerce or in business, may be familiar with the theory of "luck." In some cases "luck" is defined as "when opportunity and preparation meets." This is when one will become "lucky."

With the same breath, you may hear "there's no such thing as luck" or being "lucky," that there's only "preparation for an opportunity" that comes one's way, which may appear as "luck" or being "lucky" to everyone around you. Yet, many may be unaware of the subtle 20 percent preparation steps or effort that one has been performing over time. Of these two definitions given I have to agree with the latter, as there is no such thing as "luck" or one being "lucky" in life.

In everything created there must be "preparation (time) prior to the demonstration." In the case of business, this preparation, prior to the demonstration, is simply termed the "opportunity" you have prepared for over time, which most may refer to as "luck" or being "lucky." In actuality, a person who spends the needed time as well as the effort (not forcing) building the needed faith and belief in their business or their enlightened dream of a business is, in fact, doing the preparation, steps 1 and 2. He may find himself initially without any means, aside from his own enlightenment of his dreams. He goes about starting simply where he is, with whatever means he has available to him. He builds over time a faith in that enlightened dream prior to that dream's demonstration, despite not knowing how or when that dream will occur. This is the same method that Jesus used, as accounted in the Bible, when he fed the multitudes of people with only five loaves of bread and two fish. Accounts of this story state there was said to have been a lot of "preparation prior to the demonstration." This preparation of which they were speaking was actually the time spent (over time) building up a firm faith belief, and conviction in that envisioned dream (mentally, spiritually, and emotionally) of feeding the mass of people physically as well as spiritually, prior to that vision's timeless manifestation of there being enough food, even with a surplus left over, to feed every single person.

Another prime example of this, although I don't know the full details of the story, is the story of Oprah Winfrey as a little black girl growing up in the deep south of Mississippi. She over time would envision herself on the front of a national magazine *Vanity Fair* I believe it may have been a dream which later came to pass for her. The enlightenment she had, in actuality, was the first dream-creation step in process. Everything that happened over time after that was simply an ongoing building of faith, belief, and convictions in her mind mentally, spiritually, and emotionally. This building of faith and belief simply over time led to her emotions, then thereafter to her actions in life. Her firm building of belief and faith attracted to her places, people, and events, which was that same "law of attraction" mentioned earlier, in process. Everything after that, of course, we know is now history. To further demonstrate this dream preparation process in effect: I once met a lady who was a very adept Massage Therapist, working at a well-known spa and resort in the Palm Springs area, where I often receive my massages. As I lay totally relaxed on the table receiving a massage, she and I engaged in light conversation. I randomly shared with her some of these key laws that I am now sharing in this book. She became overly excited. Then she eagerly began to reveal to me how she had actually used these same three steps, shown earlier, without her being aware of it at the time, to lose weight. She related how she had lost over one hundred pounds and, as a result, was now physically fit and working in the beauty and health industry, which had always been her dream.

She shared she had lost the unwanted weight simply by deciding to do so, because she no longer liked her life or her lifestyle as an obese woman. She also revealed to me she had many times quietly pondered the thought over time in her mind of losing weight. (In actuality, she had been "seeking The Kingdom" for her dream.) She then related how she would often over time picture herself as a thin and physically fit person in her mind. She said she would often over time ponder and feel all the pleasures she would derive from being this slender and healthy person. She said that she had vividly over time seen, and happily envisioned in her own mind, herself as a thin and physical fit person way before it ever physically occurred. (She was building over time a mental, spiritual, and emotional equal for her dream first in her mind). When she did quickly begin to lose the unwanted weight, it was not a surprise to her at all. Why? Because She had physically over time begun to prepare by acting "as though" she were that thin person she had wished and envisioned herself to become way before it physically happened in her life. She had over time actually built a firm spiritual equal for her dream first in her mind. She had simply over time prepared and performed all of the two key preparation steps, and her job at that point was complete. She had already firmly built in her mind, a mental, spiritual, and emotional equal for her desired dream weight. She had built her dream in her mind first, then thereafter on the outside in her life. This accounts for why it wasn't any big surprise to her when she did physically begin to lose the weight, As she had already (mentally, spiritually, and emotionally) effortlessly built the same spiritual equal for that physical dream in her "mind" first before it ever tangibly manifested for her.

If anyone is looking for their enlightened dreams to begin effortlessly manifesting, simply preparing and using this key effort of applying this beautiful "Law of Creation," over time in their lives will definitely give them way more of whatever they're looking for in life, with less of any of their efforts.

CHAPTER 6: THE LAW OF RELATIVITY

As we leave the chapter "In the Beginning," it seems only appropriate to go into the spiritual "Law of Relativity," which is, in fact, a beautiful accompany to this Law of Creation that we have just covered. You have been shown thus far in this book, subliminally, that you already have within yourself 20 percent of what will give you the 80 percent or more of the results you're looking for in life. Your "mind," the place which all dreams are dreamt, is in essence the only key 20 percent more effort that you will have to seek or use in your life. This is what will give you 80 percent or more of what you're looking to have and achieve in life. Yes, your mind is a powerful tool you can use to visualize and thereafter create the world of your dreams.

The Law of Relativity has to do with "perception" or what is "relative," what some schools of thought refer to as a "paradigm," another 20 percent more effort which will provide you greater results in your life. One's perception of things in the outer world, or the way one sees or perceives their own world is what's relative to them. We perceive our world through our sensory organs, such as our sight, our smell, our taste, our hearing, and our touch. Those of us in the medical field refer to these sensory organs as the visual, olfactory, gressorial, audio, and tactile senses. These are all the five sensory organs in which we all perceive and interpret our external physical world.

As we interpret the world through these organs, we will individually, subconsciously, cipher and interpret what we perceive, all based on where our thoughts and our attention is placed at that given time of our experiences. This is referred to as our perception of the world around us, or what may be referred to as "how one sees the world" or how it's relative to them. It is important to note that no one, although we may all interpret the world through the same sensory channels and organs, as noted above, none of us truly perceive the world the same way. That's one of the reasons why we are referred to as "individuals."

Yes, two people may look at the same identical thing. They may see a picture or sunset, or they may hear a sound, taste a piece of food, smell a rose, or feel a touch. However, none of us, although we experience the same things, will, in essence, always see or interpret it the same way. This is mainly because of where our conscious, as well as our unconscious focus (thoughts and attention), is placed at the time of our experiences.

This law of Relativity in "practical" thinking is basically saying that "nothing in this world which occurs is good or bad," but it's our perception or our paradigms that makes it relative or "so" to us. This "so," or what's "relative" to us, is what also makes it "good or bad" to us. Yes, it is our thinking and our perception (our paradigms) of how we interpret situations or events in our life that makes it good or bad to us, not the events themselves. This is the reason why people's opinions vary. This may further account for why our responses, reactions, as well as our behavior, which we will be covering in the preceding chapter entitled "Dream Attitude," towards what happens to us in life may also gravely vary. It's because of our perception of that particular event, situation, or condition, and what it means to us is also different, all based on where our focus, attention, and our thoughts are placed at that given time. A perfect illustration of how we perceive or how our perception varies in any particular situation is how one may think after the result of losing their job. If one interprets this event or situation as a "bad thing" happening in their life, their thoughts thereafter will be that of negativity, which will take them directly away from their dreams.

If someone else placed in this same identical situation sees or interprets this event as a "good thing" happening in their life that may be an opportunity for something even better, which has to do with the law of "sacrificing and unification" that we will be discussing in a later chapter, their perception of this

event will be "good", and their thoughts thereafter will be
that of "good," positive, or right consciousness, which will
again take them directly to their dreams.

It's important to note here that where one's thoughts and
attention (their focus) is placed at the time of any event will
greatly determine their perceptions of any situation or event.
Because everyone's thoughts, as well as where their attention
lies, varies, so will their individual perceptions (paradigm)
vary. A prime example of this would be the perceptions of
two people witnessing the same auto accident at the time of
its occurrence, and why their perception and subsequent report of what occurred in the accident would vary greatly, all
as a result of simply where their attention and thoughts, their
focus, was placed at the time the accident occurred.

One individual may report the light was green when the
car entered the intersection. Another individual, viewing the
same accident, may report the light was yellow when the car
entered the intersection. Their accounts, although different
from what they each said occurred, was all simply based
on where their thoughts, attention, and focus was placed at
the time the accident occurred. One viewer's attention may
have been on one thing, say both the cars when the accident occurred, and the other viewer's attention and thought
may have been on the signal light. In this case neither party
is "right or wrong," yet it's their perception of that event
which "makes" it "right or wrong" or relative to them in
their minds, all based on where their focus (attention and
thoughts) were placed at the time the accident occurred. This
accounts for why our focus does have a strong input on the
directions of our dreams in life. So it may follow that if your
thoughts and attention are always focused mainly on our enlightened dreams in life, your perception of events that occur
in your life may be greatly different from those in life whose
thoughts and attention are not focused on their dreams.

Yes, it is always one's before and afterthoughts and their
focus (their thinking and attention before and after an event
or situation) that this 20 percent effect guides their dreams

and makes it "so" to them in their lives, not the actual events themselves. One's thinking, whether that of "good" or "bad," after and before an event, is what (as shown in chapter 3) leads to their emotions, feelings, and their mental state. Whether that mental state is good or bad is what causes their reactions, choices, behaviors in their lives. These all stems from their paradigms or perception of things in their lives, which ultimately will take them directly to their dreams, or deters and takes them directly away from their dreams (as will be shown to you in "The Law of Cause and Effect" in Chapter 16). All this again is based on where their thinking is, which all stems from what was relative to them in their lives.

Yes, one's thoughts may take them towards their dreams, or take them away from their dreams. As noted in the order of hierarchy, as shown earlier, it all started with their thoughts. Yes, one's perception of things in their lives only with proper "right consciousness" or positive thinking pertaining to anything about their dreams are of utmost importance.

I'd like you to note here that our perceptions of life and of ourselves also attracts or deters our relationships with the opposite sex as well. We do, in essence, attract who we are or who we perceive ourselves to be. Based on whether we perceive ourselves as "good" or "bad," we will in essence attract the same. When two people see or perceive the world the same or have similar paradigms, similar perceptions, and focus (thoughts and attention), they are able to blend their lives and similarities for a dream together. That's why you hear the old cliché that "similarities blend, and opposites attract," as related in Chapter 4. This also denotes if one sees or perceives themselves in any bad or negative way this little 20 percent affect, they, too, will in fact attract the same (a bad relationship), which does not serve their dreams in life.

Again, this takes us back, as always, to the first law, "Seek First the Kingdom," this little 20 percent more effort is what we must first perform, in order to perceive or see ourselves first in "right" perception. We're seeking to know and to perceive ourselves correctly in our own mind. This has to be done first, before anything or anyone else is added to us. This basically says that instead of looking for the right person first in our lives one simply "becomes that right person first" in their own lives. "Know thyself" and the correct perception of yourself first before anyone else is added to you.

Yes, all of us perceive our individual world through our "five senses," these lower faculties, as shown earlier, through our vision, our smell, our taste, our hearing, and touch. Yet, what I would like for you to discern here is that your dreams are not created or brought forth from this lower 80 percent physical plane of what you see, hear, taste, smell, or physically feel (your five senses). They are manifested and brought forth from a" higher 20 percent spiritual plane." Your dreams are brought forth through your "higher 20 percent faculties," which are your invisible spiritual faculties. These invisible faculties and preceptors, whom your mind uses to control and bring forth your dreams, are:

1. Your Intuition
2. Your Imagination
3. Your Perception
4. Your Memory
5. Your Reasoning

These five intangible 20 percent faculties or sensors that I will refer to as your "20 percent Mental Spiritual Faculties," are the non-visible faculties we all individually use to unconsciously create our dreams in life. Yes, it is our higher, non-tangible, mental and spiritual faculties that are the true channels in which we bring our dreams into existence in our lives. It is our "intuition" or our mental instinctive feeling, our "imagination" or mental vision, our "perception" or the way we mentally perceive or see things, our "memory" or our (mental) recall of things and events, and our "reasoning" or our (mental) judgment, problem-solving, or decision-making of things. Yes, it's these five mental higher 20 percent spiritual faculties that we all use to bring our dreams into play and existence in our lives.

When we separate or turn away from the "physical world" or our conscious world, which we perceive through our lower five senses just discussed, we then turn on our other higher mental (20 percent) invisible faculties and preceptors to bring our dreams into manifestation in our life. Again, this is only done, as discussed in Chapter 3, by quieting the mind and connecting with that source in order to connect with those higher spiritual faculties that are within you, called "The Kingdom."

This is the reason for mediation and/or prayer, and may account for why you see many successful people in business stepping away from all the physical activity and going within to connect with these higher faculties. They know that they must separate. This may be by way of performing daily quiet mediation or silent prayer ritual, taking a mental vacation in order to quiet their mind and connect with spirit, their subconscious faculties, or mind. They perform these things on an ongoing and consistent basis. For, in actuality, they are mentally on vacation. They're vacating their minds to separate themselves from the physical world in order to connect with their higher spiritual faculties (those faculties listed earlier). This is where most people will have their ideas revealed to them simply because they have separated from the physical world and quieted their minds to connect with their spiritual subconscious faculties. This is what effortlessly manifests their dreams in their lives. This is what all great inventors in history, including Edison, Marconi, and Einstein, have done to arrive at their ideas, inventions, and to solve vexing complex problems. Many stories of these great inventors have all noted that they tapped into their subconscious mind by stepping away from the problems they were facing, quieting their minds to connect with the subconscious mind for many great science discoveries or answers to complex problems en route to their inventions. One of the most amazing examples of this was in the life of the celebrated chemist Friedrich August Kekule von Stradonitz. He had been struggling for a long time to understand the chemical structure of a gas called benzene, which is a compound that contains six atoms of carbon and six of hydrogen. He was constantly perplexed by this problem; all his efforts had led him nowhere. Tired, exhausted, and unable to solve this complex problem, he simply stepped away and turned the problem over to his subconscious mind. Shortly after, as he was about to board a bus in London, his subconscious mind presented his conscious mind with a sudden flash. In his mind he saw an image of a snake biting its own tail and turning around like a pinwheel. This message from his subconscious mind led him to the now-known discovery of the circular arrangement of atoms that we know of as the "benzene ring."

He may have consciously, or unconsciously, been aware of the process he used to arrive at his outcome. It is said that if one simply steps away, performing this little 20 percent more effort or activity, from his daily activities to connect with spirit or his subconscious faculties, he will be three times more effective in his endeavor or work than he would have been if he would have not done so. In actuality, he's deriving the 80 percent from his 20 percent effort, which is stepping away to connect with his spiritual faculties.

This is very hard to do when we're caught up on a lower "physical" plane, but being a student of this book, you now see the importance of doing whatever you need to do to quiet the mind, separate and connect with those higher spiritual faculties to manifest your dreams. I find myself on an ongoing basis separating myself from the physical world and going within via daily silent prayer and meditation. Many times I just take a vacation or trip alone somewhere, without anyone else. Initially, I didn't know why I would find myself doing this, and needless to say, others in my life did not always understand my actions either, but the end result was I found myself being much more efficient and effective in the quest of my dreams, goals, and objectives in life. Others I know of accomplish this act of separation by taking nature walks alone, by putting themselves in any quiet nature environments, or by breaking away from their day for a fifteen-minute mediation or catnap. How can anyone, in actuality, separate from the 80 percent physical world that we perceive through our lower five senses, as previously discussed, and connect with their higher powers if there's not quietness, which is what's truly needed when one is connecting with their higher spiritual faculties?

Yes, it is these higher mental faculties that bring our true dreams into realization in our lives. As I had you recall in Chapter 4 a time back in your life when you had a dream manifest for you, a toy that you possibly dreamt of as a child that was brought into existence for you, a business that came into existence for you, a relationship, career, increased health, or whatever that dream was that came about effortlessly for you, note that it was these higher 20 percent mental spiritual faculties (preceptors) of the mind, which we have just spoken about, playing their part in bringing those dreams into tangible existence for you.

Yes, it was your intuition, your imagination, your perception, your memory, and your reasoning, all these higher mental 20 percent faculties working in synergy to bring those dreams into existence for you, simultaneously, as you were building a firm faith and belief in those dreams enlightened to you. This all denotes that you can start with absolutely nothing! I mean, with absolutely no physical means at all in your life, your dreams can still over time become a manifestation and real physical realization in your life, all by simply tapping into and activating those key 20 percent spiritual channels you have available to you.

Those beautiful dreams that you have for yourself will automatically come into play and into existence, and there's very little for you to do. All the beautiful laws being presented in this book will go to work to bring those dreams effortlessly into existence for you.

Dream Workshop:
Part I

CHAPTER 7:
WORKSHOP INTRODUCTION

My writing style in the following three chapters, as well as the physical setting will now change dramatically, becoming much more informal and relaxed over time, as you are no longer just merely sitting alone in a quiet place reading this book I have written. But, you are now perched in a seat awaiting the commencement of a one-day spiritual psychology "Dream It First Workshop," one of the same I have personally conducted to numerous audiences where they gathered together for a couple of hours to learn the effortless paths to manifesting their dreams and goals in life.

Note here that the only difference between the actual workshops I physically conduct and the one in this book that you're now reading is that there's no mentioning by name the "80/20 Law" or any of the other spiritual laws shown to you in this book. However, your keen insight and knowledge that has thus far been given to you in this book is sufficient to help you now see many of these laws in full action in your own daily life.

SO, DREAMERS WITHOUT FURTHER ADO LET'S GET STARTED!

The price that you have paid for this workshop is just the mere purchase of this book that you're now reading. This denotes the "80/20 Law" being in effect here, as in truth approximately 80 percent or more of what you are looking for in life in terms of personal growth will come from not 100 percent of the books and workshops you will read or attend in life, but from a mere 20 percent or less of the books and the workshops you will or have attended, as shown to you earlier in Chapter 2.

The only key things and materials you will actually need or have to do to complete this effortless workshop that prepares you for your dreams in life will be your willingness to read the workshop portions of this book out loud to yourself, your work manual and dream diary (located in Chapter 15 of this book), a yellow highlight pen, a pen or pencil, and several 3x5 (lined or unlined) index cards, along with all your enlightened, or non-enlightened dreams possibly buried deep within you awaiting their full physical manifestation. "So, dreamers, gather these key materials, and let's get started!"

DREAM IT FIRST
WORKSHOP: PART I
"DREAM SCPULTURE"
Workshop's Coach/Facilitator
Jacqueline Robertson

Good day! I have an exciting workshop prepared, for those of you here today! This workshop that you're about to embark on is a three-part "Dream System" that you can easily begin using today, without any force, which will immensely now in a short time frame change the negative results you're possibly getting which you have actually over time in your life allowed, even without your awareness, to delay you in turbo-boosting into existence many of your dreams and goals in life. This will all now mysteriously begin to happen over a short time period now in your life with you using none of your own efforts.

So, dreamers without further ado let's get started!

My name is Jacqueline Robertson, as per the introduction given to you earlier; however, I know that many of you here often refer to me as "The Dream Sister." Others audiences I spoken to have called me the "Dream Manifestation Expert." Why? Because I know that the entire secret to every aspect of your life, I mean, every single aspect of your life, has to do with a little effort that you refer to as "dreaming" or simply your goals in life.

I know, in fact, if you or anyone else sitting here in this room today doesn't have a bigger dream in life, bigger than those nightmares that you're possibly experiencing, then those unwanted nightmares, believe it or not, are the dreams you're surely over the time in your life going to have to take with you. Yes, every single one of you sitting in this room today is, in fact, simply dreaming. Yet many of you, I know for sure, are indeed possibly dreaming a "bad dream" or some nightmare that you desperately, desperately just want to wake up from and totally get rid of, but you're not quite sure how to accomplish this daunting task. Some of you, I'm sure, may even feel your own personal nightmares you're experiencing in your lives right now is quite different from everyone else's "dream," and that yours couldn't possibly change or get any better, and that most likely you're going to have to keep just making do with these nightmares that you're experiencing.

I even know for sure that many of you are saying, certain situations or even some supposedly key people in your life have led you to these unwarranted nightmares you're currently experiencing. Regardless of all the stuff you're possibly thinking right now, what I would like for you to do is to take a few moments and go to the second page in your dream workshop manual.

Now that you've done this, I want you to simply write a list of key things that you feel have led you to these unwarranted nightmares in your life.

SO, DREAMERS, LET'S DO THIS NOW!

Of course, you know where you currently are in these nightmares, because you've just written down all the apparent events and the circumstances surrounding those nightmares. Maybe you have written about the key people in your life that have possibly helped lead you to these unwanted dreams and nightmares you're experiencing. Possibly you have written about the key things that have recently happened to you in your life, or you've written about those things that have happened in your past. Perhaps you have written about the key choices you have made over the key years in life or the lack of key money, time, or other resources you do not presently have or haven't accumulated over time in your life. Regardless of all this "junk" that you've just written down, what I want you to know is "You can begin to live your dreams!" This is regardless of all those key things you have just written down. Your enlightened key dreams can and will in a short time become a physical realization and manifestation in your life. Believe it or not, you can have many of those key dreams you hold by simply releasing only one of those nightmares or bad dreams you have just written down. I'll show you how.

Again, it's not based on any of the things you've just written about. It doesn't matter if you're written about all the time you have wasted over the key time in your life, the key people who have recently mistreated you, or not having the key or perfect amount of health, time, money, or education you think you need. It doesn't even matter if you've written about the nightmares of a recent failed key relationship, or the pain of recently losing a key and significant loved one in your life. It doesn't matter if you've written about being bankrupt, foreclosed on, unemployed, or just being released from the hospital or even jail! None of these nightmares you have experienced over the time in your life matters at all.

You see, there's a truth that I'd like to share with you here before we begin this workshop. That truth is this: Any dreams over time you can mentally conceive, emotionally feel, and spiritually believe over time, you can and must achieve! The reason for this is that your "Your Higher Power," God, would have never allowed you to have or initially conceive any of your dreams or goals, if you weren't able or capable of receiving and, thereafter, effortlessly carrying them forth in your life. So with this you must know if your dreams or goals are just maintained long enough over time mentally, emotionally, and spiritually in your mind, even if they're mentally feared or either revered in your mind, they must and will come to pass!

You see any dream, good or bad, that's mentally, emotionally, and spiritually held just long enough in your own mind over time, must mysteriously over that time seep into your "subconscious mind." That's part of you that never sleeps. It's a part of you that was implanted within you by our "Higher Power" when you were created. This mysterious key force within you, believe it or not, is what controls all of your automatic body functions, your breathing, your heartbeat, your assimilation, and digestion of food. Even when you're asleep, it will work to maintain or manifest any of your dreams (bad or good) in your life.

In the medical field this "subconscious mind" is simply referred to as the key autonomic, or the "involuntary" system, because it will automatically work for you and was initially programmed to work for you throughout your life. In other walks of life that you may, or may not, be familiar with, this subconscious mind is referred to as a key "Law," "Force," "Power," "Spirit," "Energy," or "Higher Intelligence," and some will only refer to it as "God's key spirit, force, or power" in action. Yet, whatever you choose to call this key, you can use it over time in your life to realize your true intended dreams. What I'll be referring to it as in this (spiritual psychology) workshop today is the "subconscious mind" working, as instructed by you over time, to release or manifest into existence any dream or nightmare that you desire or wish to totally get rid of or release from your life. Believe it or not, this key "subconscious mind" knows the answer to all our problems when we instruct it to solve any problems in our lives, despite our not knowing how or when it will happen.

I am sure that, with all life's unexpected key problems, nightmares, challenges, changes or unexpected stuff happening or possibly occurring right now in your life, it may, in fact, be very difficult for you to consciously stay focused on any dreams. You can easily, without your own awareness, get off-track over time with just only your own "conscious" "will power," and not turning these things over to your subconscious mind to solve automatic for you.

In fact, what anyone truly needs to stay focused on any anything in life over time, including their dreams, are keys or tools. Tools are needed in order to more effortlessly perform any tasks in life. Many of you, I'm sure, may attend a religious gathering, or you may possibly read your Bible or other self-help or business books. Why? Because you over time have used these key things as your tools to help you stay focused on, or in concurrency, with your beliefs, so that you can more easily incorporate those same beliefs or knowledge into your daily life, which will ultimately lead to your actions and ultimately your dreams in life.

If you had a goal of losing weight, you may utilize walking, exercising, or dieting as a key tool to help you accomplish this task over time. What happens if you go several months without attending your church or reading? You would simply, over a short period of time, lose sight or focus on those previously built beliefs. What happens if you go several months without walking, exercising, or watching the foods you consume? You would slowly lose your previous build, focus, as well as the gains you had previously, right? So as we all need key tools to stay focused and accomplish our goals in life, we also need them to help us stay focused and accomplish our dreams in life.

As mentioned earlier, it's very difficult to stay focused on any dream with only "conscious" effort or simple "will power" without using the "subconscious mind" as a very important and vital key tool in our lives. One key and effective tool that I'll be showing you how to use in today's workshop, in order to help you stay focused on all your enlightened dreams and goals in life, by using your "subconscious mind" is what I call

"DREAM PHOTOGRAPHING."

With dream photographing you're simply taking a personal mental photograph or snapshot of your dreams, then, thereafter, using that same snapshot or photograph to bring those dreams into full focus, clarity, and full spectrum in your life. What you're actually doing is implanting over time your dreams into your "subconscious mind," so that "involuntary system" I just spoke of earlier can eagerly go to work on bringing your enlightened dreams effortlessly into realization in your life, even without you being aware of the process or how it's happening. Soon thereafter invisible vibrations will begin to be set up, gradually, without any work on your behalf, mysteriously attracting everything needed in life to bring forth those dreams, whatever they are for you, into a real physical manifestation in your life.

This is often referred to as that mystic key "Law of Attraction," or what some may refer to as a "force," "energy," "spirit," "power," or either "God" mysteriously working in your life. Your dreams will definitely be happening. You'll be mysteriously at or in the right place, at the right time, saying and doing the right things without any conscious control or will power about yourself at all. Why? Because this will be that "involuntary system," your "subconscious mind" working on your behalf to manifest those intended dreams into life for you.

Dream photographing is easily accomplished by you simply writing out your dream(s) on paper. As instructed in the Bible where it states "Write your vision on a table," Habakkuk: 2:2, this means to simply write it down! When you're writing out your dreams, they must possess the "Three Ps," meaning your dream must be sculptured and written in the following fashion: They must be written in the "present" (tense), they must be written in the first person, or from a "personal" perspective, and finally they must be written in a "positive" form, or format. This is what's meant in the same verse (after you've written it on a table) "Make it loud and clear," Habakkuk: 2:2.

THREE EASY STEPS TO
SCULPTURING YOUR DREAMS

If your dream is to purchase a new home, you would make this statement "loud and clear" by sculpturing your dream using the following three steps:

Step 1: Your Dream must be written as though it's presently happening. An example of this would be "I have a new home." It's sculptured and written in the present tense, as though it's already happening now in your life. Why? Because the "subconscious mind" (like a robot) does not process future or past information, or events, it only takes present-day commands from you. The picture that you'll be implanting into your subconscious mind has to be a present-day picture. This has to happen in order for your subconscious robot to follow your commands.

2. Your dream must be made "personal." It's not about "us" or "we," it's only about "you." So, with this in mind, when you're writing out your dream, you must use the word "I," because this "dream" is your dream, no one else's dream. Someone other than you may also have this same dream, but this dream has been enlightened just for you. Because of this, you want to always utilize the word "I" when you're writing and sculpturing your dreams so your 'subconscious mind" can go to work on that dream especially for you.

3. Your dream must be "positive." You want to positively assert the truth about your dream, making it loud and clear. You're not going to use negative words when you're writing out your dreams in life, words that lack 'faith," such as "I wish I could buy a home," "One day I'll have a home," or "I'm hoping to buy a home some day." These statements do not indicate a strong "belief," or "faith." You're going to be positively asserting the truth about your dreams in the "affirmative" by making such statements as "I have a new home!" or "I'm buying a new house!"

Now your dream is sculptured and being prepared for its physical manifestation it has the "three Ps." It's in the present tense, it's personal, and it's positive. It has been made "loud and clear" because this is the way the "subconscious mind" (your robot) will photograph and thereafter perceive that picture of your dream, so it can then go to work on that picture for you. In conjunction with these "three Ps," your dreams have to be specific and in full detail. Again, this is because your subconscious mind only deals with precise, "loud and clear" information. If this is the case, your dream needs be specific, clear in detail, and form. For example, "I have a beautiful four-bedroom, three-bath, 2,800 square-foot home with a sunken Jacuzzi tub, by December 31, 2013." Now your dream is specific and in full detail, coupled with those "three Ps," all prepared for your subconscious robot to receive your command.

I would like for you to now take a few minutes to sculpture your own dreams. This can be anything that you want in your life right now. It can be any item. It may be the quest for a soul mate. It may be an increased spiritual life. It even may be a new car or career. Whatever those dreams are for you, I want you to go to the third page in your Work Manual now, and write down your enlightened dreams you personally have for your life. Remember, they must be "Loud and Clear," "Specific and Detailed," and they must be sculptured to include "The three Ps."

SO, DREAMERS, LET'S GET STARTED!

Now your dream is all sculptured. It has the three Ps, as mentioned earlier, and it's "loud and clear" and sculptured in full detail. The next thing I'll be showing you now is how to work your camera to bring your dream into full focus for its physical manifestation. You will learn how to incant those dreams you have just finished sculpturing. Incant means to state something repetitively, with intense feelings and enthusiasm.

For example, have you ever lost your car keys and while looking everywhere for them, you find yourself saying, "I

can't find them! I can't find them! I just cannot find them!"
What you're unconsciously doing is incanting this statement. You're stating it repetitively, you're repeating it over
and over again, and you're repeating it with intense feeling
and enthusiasm. That's the reason why you can't find those
keys, because you have sunken this information (unbeknown
to yourself) into your subconscious mind, instructing and
programming it "not to locate your keys."

Now you're going to learn to do the same with your enlightened dreams you have written down. You're going to be
repeating your dreams over and over again to yourself with
intense feelings and enthusiasm. Why? Because your subconscious mind will then perceive that picture you're con-
veying based on your beliefs and feelings about that dream.
I use the word "enthusiasm" here, because the base of the
word's (Greek) definition means the "God Within." It's imperative that you believe what you're saying from within, and
that you feel what you're saying when you're repeating it.
You can't be a monotone broken record repeating something

over and over without feelings, because, if that's the case, the subconscious mind will only perceive it that way, and will not be able to cipher and assimilate the information you're wanting to convey to it, and will not, thereafter, be able go to work in bringing that dream into a physical realization or manifestation in your life.

Now your dream is all set up. It consists of the 'Three Ps." It's in the present tense, it's personal, and it's positive. And it's also specific in full detail, and you are now incanting that dream.

Now I'm going to show you how to actively work that dream to aid you into finally bringing it into a true physical realization or manifestation in your life. Remember here that you're not going to know how or when this dream is going to come into existence. You're not going to know the gestation period. The one thing you must know and believe is that your dream will come to pass.

Now that you have your dreams almost finally prepared, you will learn now how to work that dream. The most successful way to do this is to implant that dream, or your dreams that you have for yourself, on 3x5 index cards that you have brought to class with you. If you have several dreams, you want to write out each dream on a separate index card. You're going to carry these index cards around any way that is accessible for you, in your purse, maybe in your wallet, your pocket, or your notebook. Again, it doesn't matter which method you use. Any way that these cards can always be accessible to you on an ongoing daily basis will work, until your dream is physically manifested.

I like to recommend just a little more effort in accomplishing this task by you simply purchasing a small photograph album, which you can purchase at any convenience store, Wal-Mart, or Walgreen's photo department. The cost of this album is little, only about 99 cents. Instead of inserting your personal photographs into each sleeve of your album, you're going to be implanting your 3x5 index cards. These are your "Dream Photographs" and will now be your own personal and key "Dream Photo Album."

What you're doing with these 3x5 index cards is using them as "key tools," as I previously showed you, to build up faith and belief in your dreams. You're going to now repeat these dreams on your cards to yourself four times a day, or at breakfast, lunch, dinner, and more importantly, prior to sleep. It is a known fact that prior to sleep you are in a semi-hypnotic state, and your subconscious mind at that time is more receptive to the suggestions of your dreams and your thoughts, because your five physical senses are less tuned in. With this in mind, your subconscious mind can more easily and readily go to work on bringing your dreams into physical form in your life. However, if you choose to use this key as a tool you must not disclose to anyone your dreams you have written down, until they have been manifested or have come to pass in your life.

Dream photographing is a secret key for you to begin using today in your life, to over time bring any of your enlightened dreams into a real physical realization, and this is regardless of whatever that dream is. "Dream Photographing" has worked for me consistently throughout my life, and I have, and still do, use this silent little tool to obtain many of my dreams that have been enlightened to me, such dreams as increasing a personal relationship, obtaining a career dream, or any other dreams or goal I may have.

I'll share with you a personal story that I'm sure many of you may be able relate to. Quite a few years ago, I had a very unfavorable encounter with a woman on my job that had left me with very harsh and adamant feelings towards her. As a result of this, I over time had developed an adamant dislike for this woman. Just the mere thought or any mentioning of her name would cause me to have "tension and stress." Yet, in truth, I really didn't like those feelings, and how I was allowing it to affect me. I reluctantly decided to utilize this "Dream Photographing" technique in order to accomplish my dream of, at the least, having some type of favorable feelings towards her. So I wrote on a 3x5 index card this painstaking statement: "I have a congenial relationship with Margaret." I then wrote on another card this following statement: "Margaret and I get along just fine." Now you must know it was very difficult for me to write these two statements initially, because I had no conscious positive thoughts, love, or good feelings towards this person at all, considering the ugly thing I felt she had done to me, yet I gave it the benefit of the doubt, and I continued to repeat these uncanny dreams from my 3x5 index cards four times a day with conviction. I repeated these statements several times to myself upon awaking each morning, prior to having lunch and dinner and before falling to sleep each night.

I repeated these dreams with intense feelings, enthusiasm, belief, and convictions. Slowly over a short period of time (approximately 20 days), believe it or not, the adamant feelings towards Margaret just dissipated, without my awareness of how or when it all had occurred. I recall walking down the hall one day, and she was walking towards me. Normally I would ditch her, and go in the opposite direction in which she was approaching. If I couldn't avoid her totally and was forced to walk past her, I would always act as though I had tunnel vision and would look straight through her, not even acknowledging her presence.

As I was passing her one day in the corridor, the strangest thing happened. I found myself staring directly at Margaret, and without any control about myself, I said to her, with a big smile on my face, "Hello, Margaret, how are you?" And I continued to walk past her as though nothing had ever happened between us. Believe me when I say this, I was shocked beyond belief! And so was she. I was truly amazed at my uncanny ability to release those long-held harsh feelings I had towards Margaret. The desired dreams I had written down had indeed over time sunken into my subconscious mind, and in a short period of time had me carrying out these mysterious actions.

Believe me, when I say this, this is what this "Dream Photographing" will do for you in your life. You can have whatever it is you want. Your dreams will become a realization in your life. What you're actually doing is simply imitating how many "Master Painters" have arrived at such beautiful works of art. When Van Gogh, one of the "Masters," was asked, "How have you been able to paint such beautiful paintings?" his response was "I simply dream my paintings (first), and then I paint my dreams."

PART II
DREAM TALK

CHAPTER 8:
THE DREAM WORKSHOP

What we will be looking at in this second part of today's workshop is called "dream talk," and how you will now take your sculptured dreams you have molded and now begin over time communicating those dreams to yourself on a daily basis. Why? Because as you will now see, how you communicate those dreams over time to yourself is going to determine the directions of those dreams.

SO, DREAMERS, LET'S GET STARTED!

In my childhood, I was diagnosed with having a fairly severe hearing and speech impediment. Because I had a hard time hearing the words that were spoken to me, I also had a hard time imitating the words. When I would speak, the words I attempted to verbalize would come out flat, harsh, and very much unarticulated. I remember in the second, or maybe it was possibly the third grade them taking me out of the classroom and enrolling me in a speech therapy class. The speech therapist would work with me on my linguistic skills, my enunciation, pronunciation, and articulation of words. This went on for several years, semester after semester, year after year until I reached a "plateau," whatever that was, I didn't know at the time. Then they decided to enroll me in another form of speech therapy where I would learn to read the other person's lips, just in case I didn't hear what was being spoken to me, so I would at least get by being able to read their lips.

Following this, they wanted to fit me with a hearing aid. I had adamantly refused it. I told my mother, "No, I don't want it." Because of my refusal, the audiologist informed my parents that I would just "get by" in life. Well, indeed that's just what happened to me. "I just got by" in my life. I would always find myself trying to compensate for these deficits I had. The speech therapist had informed all my teachers to have me sit in the front rows of the classrooms, so I could hear what they're saying when teaching their class. I would often find myself asking everyone around me to repeat themselves, because I just couldn't hear or understand what was going on.

When asking people to repeat themselves became too much of an arduous, painstaking task and much too frustrating for me, because of them making fun of me or by them simply not wanting to continuously repeat themselves, I just stopped asking, which definitely affected my world, providing me little stimulation mentally and making me appear different from others in my life. This over time definitely affected me in the classroom, because it affected my ability to learn. By my having these literal physical deficits coupled with my then own self-imposed limitations, it greatly affected how I felt and thought about myself. I didn't think that I was "normal." I didn't think or feel that I was like other people. How could I? I couldn't talk, I couldn't hear, I couldn't even see, without wearing glasses.

Regardless of these nightmares occurring in my life, somewhere deep within myself I had a bigger dream and vision for my life. A bigger dream, bigger than those nightmares I was experiencing. Slowly, I began over time communicating to myself in a more positive, gentle, easy, and benign fashion, and this key began to change my life. Before this I had been very hard on myself, always beating myself up daily with negative information about myself that I would give to myself. This, along with the negative feedback that I would often get from many of the people in my life, gravely affected me. Although I had just lost both of my parents within three months apart, that same year I managed to enroll in college after graduating from high school.

I was going through a very emotional and painful time in my life, all while I was still trying to build faith and confidence in myself as a young eighteen-year-old with no parental support or guidance. As I entered my first year of college, I saw that I was one of only four other blacks in the entire program. This was foreign to me at that time, since the schools I had attended in grade and secondary school were primary black institutions. I remember the Acting Chairperson over the Occupational Therapy curriculum I was majoring in calling me in to her office, after my questioning a final term grade that I did not feel I merited, to tell me (not about the grade I didn't merit, and I was now asking about) that the chairperson, who had supposedly just left for a one-year sabbatical leave and who could not apparently be reached, had left specific instructions in her black grade book. Her instructions were not to allow me to continue in the program. When I nervously inquired as to why I wouldn't be allowed to continue, I was informed, somewhat reluctantly by her, that it was because my speech and English wasn't good or up to par for their program. I remember looking stung and confused with tears swelling up in my eyes, and I recall saying to her, through the rolling tears down my face, in my "flat, unarticulated voice" at the time, "Who are you... to tell me... what I can't do?" "Even if I can't speak the way you think I should doesn't have anything to do with me learning!" I indeed had apparently already built a bigger dream for myself, much bigger than this apparent nightmare that she was

now talking about. I had, in fact, without my own awareness over time had built a dream much greater for my life,
greater than my past and, yes, certainly larger than what she
was now telling me, and I wasn't about to allow her or the
chairman who had left those biased instructions to take my
dreams away from me. Needless to say, despite the instructions left in that little black book by the chairman, I was still
there, to her astonishment, after she did finally return from
her one-year, supposedly, sabbatical leave. Of course she,
and the acting Chair before her, made sure that there was
always some reason for me to repeat every class in that core
program, although I was making above-average grades in all
the other non-core classes that they did not teach. This continued until I took my final core class taught by an unbiased
instructor from a different department who passed me with
a 3.0 grade average in my finals. And I then went off for my
unpaid four-month Clinic Affiliation in the hospitals, where
I then finished both the Mental Health and Physical Disabil-
ity clinics, again, to their amazement, at the top of my class

with a 4.0 grade average, simply because they were not the ones giving out the grades! I after gradation over time went on to practice in the medical field of Occupational Therapy for twenty-one years, half of which time I functioned as a independent and sub-contractor, which was virtually unheard of by most practitioners in the field at that time. I over this same time wrote and had published in the "Occupational Therapy professional journal" an article that won third place where I was paid a writer's fee in a professional "writing contest." I over time, thereafter, opened and operated two Licensed Board and Care Facilities for ten years from the skills I had acquired in that same profession, all this while I obtained my real estate agent, and later, broker's license, notary public license, insurance license, health care administrator's license, all this again while raising a family, always finishing "top of my class" every single time whether there were "even playing grounds" or not.

This is exactly what you're also going to have to have in your life. You're going to have to identify those few key strengths you do have in your life and leverage over time that little you have and build a bigger dream for your life, bigger than any circumstance or conditions in your life, and certainly much larger then what others say or do to you in your life. By my simply identifying this key to who I really was, and then stepping out of my own fear and comfort zone and building faith and belief in myself, and learning how to communicate those same beliefs to my life, I was able to quickly over time manifest my dreams in life. By my reading books that reiterated the real truth about me and who I really was, I learned over time to think only on whatsoever was true, whatsoever was noble, whatsoever was right, whatsoever was pure, whatsoever was lovely, and whatsoever was of good report, as quoted in Philippians 4:8. For I knew if there were to be any excellence, virtue, or anything worth praising in my life, I must only think and focus on those key things. This was loudly and clearly telling me to simply transform my mind with truth, only positive and right conscious thinking, and thoughts about who I really am.

The books I read alone, along with my daily affirmations and prayers over time, became my keys I used daily at that very vulnerable and dark time in my life, to re-integrate this newfound consciousness and awareness about me. Despite all the nightmares surrounding my life, I slowly, over a short interval of time built the needed faith, belief, and convictions in and about myself to take me to all my dreams in life. I did this for myself by reading anything positive, listening to positive audio tape programs, and through my daily prayer and mediation. Of all the many tools that were available to me, they helped more to quickly accelerate the reprogramming of my mind and kept me totally focused on my dreams. There are many positive and key tools available for you to start using today! Yet, remember if you choose to use them, only identify a few that work well for you personally over a short time frame, and then put your entire weight on only those few and key ones you have identified. Do this starting today! They are:

Mediation

Prayer

Reciting affirmations

Reading positive books and materials

Listening to positive audio books

Positively talk to your self

Attending events that build you up, mentally, spiritually, and emotionally

Mental imagery

Visualization

Physically acting or playing out dreams

Posting pictures of your dream around you

Affiliating yourself only with other positive, like-minded individuals

Any few of these things you can isolate and identify over any short time frame in your life that easily fits into your present lifestyle and works well for you can then be your own keys for life. They can easily become a part of your personal lifestyle, starting today! They will then be your personal keys in life to aide you in staying consciously focused on your enlightened dreams with little effort on your part. They indeed will be the little things that will provide you much in life.

So, "Dreamers," what I would like for you to do is to stop, and go to the last page of your workshop manual, (page 6) where you will see your "Dream Diary." This is where you now record these "key tools" I have just written down.

SO, DREAMERS, LET'S DO THIS NOW!

What I found out in the midst of all those dark nightmares in my life is by using just only a few of these key tools that I had identified that worked best for me in my life at that time and what you will also find out for yourself, that I'm definitely okay, and I can do anything that I want in this life. What you will also find out, by just using any few of these tools, is it is definitely okay for you to say "I can," "I choose to," and "I will." These few "key words" are powerful tools that will take you, or anyone, anywhere they choose to go in life. They will indeed surely and quickly take you to any of your dreams you care to venture.

Did you know that numerous studies have revealed there's a big key correlation between career and financial success based on one's ability to "perfect" a powerful vocabulary. What does all of this say? Yes, communication is definitely very important. Yet, what does it say about the often and key negative communication we give to ourselves without our awareness, hundreds of times a day? Have you ever thought where does this take you in terms of your present and future dreams, and what direction you go in life? Well, negative self-talk, without you possibly being aware of it, will always take you away from your dreams in life. Yet, positive self-talk, too, without you ever being aware of it takes you directly to your dreams in life.

I mentioned in the introduction of this workshop you have the inborn, innate right and potential, and God-given right to dream, to go anywhere that you want in this world as long as you don't hurt anyone in the process. If this is our God-given right, have you ever pondered the thought of where have we gotten the negative self-talk that we give to ourselves daily?

I'm going to tell you where all this type of self-talk stems from. You see, when you were born, you didn't have a "conscious mind," meaning you didn't know the difference between right and wrong, nor did you have an awareness of what was right or wrong. What you did have was a "subconscious mind," a blank unprogrammed mind that would later be controlled over time by your "conscious mind." This key blank program (your subconscious mind) was ready to be turned or programmed by your conscious environment, or more specifically, by the key people who were in authority or anyone having control over you, namely your parents, teachers, or anyone else having full authority over you.

As you were growing up certain things were going on over time in your environment that were, in fact, programming your subconscious mind, without you ever being aware of it. Let's take a look at some of the events that were possibly happening, indeed, programming your mind. Possibly when you were learning to walk as a child, you would risk (security) taking a few steps independently, but as you performed this brave act, the first thing you heard was "Oh! Don't fall!" Possibly before that, as you were crawling around on the floor, you saw a big beautiful fire burning in the fireplace. You crawled over towards it to see what it was about, because it was so bright. As you stuck your little hand out towards the fire, the first thing you would hear was "Oh no! Don't do that! Get away from there! You'll burn yourself!"

Following that, when you did over some time learn to walk through trial and error, you would see something that looked very interesting lying on the ground, pick it up, and examine it. In examining it, you would stare at it, feel it, possibly smell it, and then possibly eat a little bit of it. Why? Because you perceived this thing you had found through some of your five senses to determine what it was. Yet, the first thing you would hear in a loud voice in the mist of your thorough examination was "Oh, no! Don't do that! Don't touch that! Put that down! That's nasty! That's not good for you!" And all of a sudden, as you heard these loud incanted shots, you would also possibly receive a little smack (a stimulus) on your hand simultaneously. Now, believe it or not, this was the way most of us were initially programmed: "You can't do this, or you can't do that."

"If you do that, that's not good for you." We were all most likely programmed with all the "nos" by the people in authority in our lives, our parents, our teachers, or others that were over or in charge us. These people in your life all had very good intentions for you, because they loved and they were basically just trying to protect you. They could really only give to you what had been given to them when they were being raised. What they didn't know is that they were over time programming you for life, programming you to say "no" to all the things you want in our life, and to say "no" to your desires.

Now you're no longer a child, but a mature, conscious-minded, adult. You now have free will and a "conscious mind" you can now use. You're now able to gather new information and new data about who you really are. You're now able to reprogram that subconscious mind and those old paradigms with your now own conscious mind, not with the minds and perceptions of those that raised you. This is what you're going to have to learn in order to reprogram your mind and manifest your dreams in life.

You heard the old saying coined after the great motivational speaker Zig Ziglar, "Garbage in, garbage out." What this is basically saying is that if you are programming garbage in, this negative stuff over time, then that's what you're going to produce in your life over time. If this is the case, how about reprogramming your subconscious mind with good stuff over time in order to have good things happen over time in your life? Why not!? Did you know that your subconscious mind, believe it or not, doesn't even know the difference between right or wrong? Why? Because it's under control of your conscious mind, so whatever you program it with or tell it to do is what it's going to do and produce for you in your life. You must remember that your subconscious mind is only a mindless robot that is (turned on and off) programmed or deprogrammed, by your conscious mind, and you are the key by your own commands telling it what it can or cannot do for you.

In your workbook there is an exercise where you will now learn how to replace this negative self-talk you have been giving to yourself with positive self-talk. You will learn how to reprogram your subconscious mind over time. In this exercise you will allow yourself to become more consciously aware of the negative terminology you're programming your subconscious mind with on a daily basis. It will also allow you to reprogram the subconscious mind with positive or right conscious information and thoughts in order to attract your dreams in life.

On page 4 of your workbook there are lines for you to do just this. Here you'll be listing the negative terminology you give to yourself. To aide you in doing this, there's a list of negative statements that we may find ourselves giving to ourselves in quest or en route to our dreams, statements such as "I can't," "I don't have the money," "I don't have the resources," "I don't know the right people," "I don't have the education," "I don't have the time," "I don't have the energy," et cetera, and all the negative walls and objections and "nos" we say to ourselves about our dreams.

Adjacent to each item on this list there are blank spaces, where you will be able to replace negative self-talk with positive self-talk. When you're filling in these spaces, you need not be concerned about the verbiage or the terminology you're using. You just want to be able to take those negative statements listed and convert them into any type of positive statements. For example, if you're telling yourself, "I don't know the right people," to turn that negative statement into a positive statement you would write, "I will meet the right people." If you're telling yourself "I don't have the education," you can replace that with "I will get the education" or "the education that I currently have is sufficient." However you choose to convert or turn around that negative statement is up to you. The important thing here is it must be converted into a positive statement. Remember, you're not concerned with how or when this positive statement will manifest or will occur in your life. Your job is to just convert the statement into any positive form.

Okay, dreamers, let's take some time and do this exercise now! Now that you have your list all written out, as you examine this list, you can now see how easy it is to learn to replace this negative self-talk with positive self-talk. Believe it or not, there are only a few key phrases that you have been using over time, without your awareness, that's actually been the kingpins keeping you away or deterring you from most of your dreams in life. What I would like for you to do is to use the yellow highlight pen you brought with you today, and I want you to simply identify by highlighting those key phrases you know for sure you are using daily in reference to any of your dreams you have for yourself.

SO, DREAMERS, LET'S DO THIS NOW!

What I want you to know that it's imperative you learn to start right now today replacing those key negative statements you're regularly using and incanting to yourself with only positive and key self-talk.

It may initially feel very uncomfortable to talk positively to yourself about your dreams in life, because you have been so conditioned and programmed over time to talk and speak negatively to or about yourselves and your dreams, but by you now being more continuously aware of the negative garbage or the key negative words that you have been feeding yourself daily, you can more easily in a short time learn to immediately replace those key negative phases with only positive statements.

In doing this you are definitely doing the best and key thing that you can possibly do for yourself in attracting your desires and dreams in your life. Eventually, it will definitely become a habit, because it's common knowledge it takes only approximately twenty to twenty-one days, give or take, to form any new habit. So don't be so hard on yourself. You will see now in a short time frame you using only positive and key statements to yourself, in your life daily as well as when you're around others.

PART III

DREAM WEAVING

CHAPTER 9:
THE DREAM WORKSHOP

Now what we're going to be looking at in this final portion of this three-part workshop today is what's referred to as "dream weaving," how you will start today weaving and integrating those enlightened dreams, into your behavior in order to turbo burst those dreams into a final manifestation in your life.

SO, DREAMERS, LET'S GET STARTED!

I'd like to share with you a very interesting, yet informative, poem. The author of this poem is unknown.

"Did you know you tell on yourself by the friends you seek, by the manner in which you speak, by the way you employ your leisure time, and by the use you make of dollar and dime? You tell on yourself by the clothes you wear, by the spirit in which your burdens bear, by the kind of things of which you laugh, by the records you play on your phonograph. You tell on yourself by the way you walk, by the things in which you are a delight to talk, by the manner in which you bear defeat, so simple as how you eat, by the books you choose from your well-built shelf in these ways, and more you tell on yourself. So there's really no particle of sense in an effort to keep a false pretense."

Again, the author of this poem is unknown.

Taking this poem into account, I'd like to share with you a very exciting, key word. The word is "praxis." If you never heard of this word before, don't worry, your next-door neighbor, or approximately 80 percent or more of people in your everyday life, may have never heard of this word either? But if you're studious like I am, and you would take the time to look up the definition of this key word, it would be simply defined as an "exercise or discipline for a specified purpose," which really doesn't say very much.

If you would take it a step further and you looked up the key word "praxeology" in your medical dictionary, you would see that word simply defined as the "study of behavior." Yet, it does go further than both of these concise definitions. You see, the word "praxis" means a mind and body exercise, or discipline. It is definitely an exercise that keeps your mind in proper alignment with your body's actions or behavior. For "praxis" is simply the "weaving and the integration of your beliefs with your behavior" in your life.

I'm quite sure your first thought may be "That's not a difficult thing for anyone to do," because everyone's belief is integrated with their behavior, isn't it? If they believe something, then that's the way they're going to act, right? Believe it or not, this is not always the case. More often than not, a person's true beliefs are not always integrated with their behavior. More often than not, when one's beliefs are integrated with their behavior, usually their belief is "false or unsound."

Because the belief they have is false and unsound, they will have a hard time getting to and maintaining their dreams in life. I'll give you an example of this. If you're in business and you feel or think that it's okay to walk over people on your way up to the top just as long as you don't step on them too hard, this belief, of course, is false and unsound. Because it's false and unsound, you're going to definitely have a hard time realizing your dream., If you do appear to get to your dream, you're going to have a hard time maintaining that dream. Yet, there are times when a person's beliefs are sound and true, but they are failing in integrating that sound belief in their behavior, hence their life.

Let me give you an illustration of this. Let me take a few minutes here and introduce you to "Brother Brown." You all know him. He's possibly your next-door neighbor, your co-worker, maybe, a business associate, a family member or friend. You see, Brother Brown, he professes and confesses all day long, sometimes even into the wee hours of the night, to be a "Christian." Yet, his belief about "Christianity" has not over time been woven into his behavior or into his life.

Let me tell you something about Brother Brown.: You see, Brother Brown, he's just a little prejudiced, because he just loves to prejudge and often talk about other people. And Brother Brown, he refuses to give his time or any of his resources to others. Now on Sunday morning when they pass that collection basket around, he puts an envelope in it all right, but it's usually only $3 hidden inside his envelope. When members of Brother Brown's congregation are not around, he has over time become really callous, abrupt, arrogant, and insensitive to the needs of others.

Now you may think he's responsible because he's at church every single Sunday, and he's always on time for choir rehearsal and Wednesday night prayer meeting. Yet, he's really not responsible at all, because he seems to be a blamer. He blames everyone and everything in sight for everything bad that happens to him. We all know if you're blaming others, then you're really not responsible. So one must know here that if they're blaming others, you really are not the responsible person they and others may think you are.

I'm quite sure you must hear people in Brother Brown's congregation whispering, unbeknownst to him, "He's not Christian. He's a big hypocrite." Why? Because Brother Brown is definitely heavily bounded, but yet he has over time become really no earthly good! Indeed, Brother Brown knows nothing about this key concept of "praxis." If he did, Brother Brown's true beliefs, that is, of Christianity, would be definitely integrated into his behavior. And there would be no doubt in Brother Brown's mind, or anyone else mind, who he really is, and he would most likely be living his true dreams.

I'm going to stop here in this workshop for a moment, and I'm going to be pretty candid and up front with you. I don't mean to hurt or be offensive to anyone here, but I'm going to share with you a key truth. For most of you, if you're not already living your true dreams in your life, it's possibly because your true beliefs about that dream and yourself over time has not been integrated with your behavior. You see, there are two key things that may be occurring in your life right now! Either that belief or paradigm about your dream or about yourself, as

I just shared with you earlier, over time has become false and unsound, and because this belief is false and unsound you're definitely having a hard time obtaining and then thereafter maintaining that dream about yourself in your life, or what's occurring in your life is that your dream or beliefs about yourself are perfectly sound and true, yet you have failed over time in integrating that sound and true belief into your behavior. So with this in mind, you're going to have to learn now how to start '"weaving and integrating" your beliefs into your behavior to manifest your dreams and goals in life.

What you've been doing over time in the past is simply telling yourself as well as others in your life that you're "believing" and thinking, since you're outwardly saying this is what you are now believing. Yet, you do not truly believe. You have not over time built up a belief in your dream or yourself. Subsequently, a real belief really hasn't happened within you. So what you're going to have to learn how to do is to go at this a little "backwards." You're going to have to learn how to start "behaving" so you can then start "believing." You heard the old saying, "Seeing something is believing it." That's because when you see or perceive something through any of your five senses, you're more prone to believe it.

With this key information I have now shared with you, what you're going to have to start doing, so you can start believing, is to right now in your life start seeing yourself as that person you want yourself to be. Because this is the way your subconscious mind will then perceive you, as only that key person, and then this is when you will actually start believing. Why? Because things will then start to happen in your physical world though the Law of Attraction, you can then see or perceive through your five senses that makes and says it is real to you. This a very powerful key principle to now prepare you for your dreams in your life referred to as "acting as though," as taught in the Bible.

With this in mind, you do have the okay to "fake it over time 'til we make it." This may sound somewhat negative, but it is definitely spiritually sound. One way to accomplish this is to start right now in your life. Yes, acting and behaving as though you're already that key person you believe yourself to be, what many will label simply as being or having self-confidence.

I'm quite sure many of you remember "Cary Grant," a very confident actor. I just loved him! He was one of my favorite actors. I thought he was so classy, so polished, and so sexy. Did you know that wasn't his real name? I believe his real name was Archibald Leach, or something to that affect. He just made the name "Cary Grant" up. You see, he wanted to be "Cary Grant" so badly, over time he would say to himself, "I'm Cary Grant" until he just started "acting and behaving" like "Cary Grant." Then he was finally able to bring Cary Grant into existence in his life.

That's what you're going to have to do or start doing right now in your life. You're going to have to start right now, today, with only the little you may have. Start acting and behaving now over the present time in your life as though you're already that key person you believe yourself to be. I know this may be a relatively new concept to most of you here, but it is a known fact that if you want a different end result in life, something different to happen in your life, you definitely have to be able to do something different in order to get that different end result.

A lot of times doing something a little differently can be your true key, and it definitely includes stepping out of fear and present comfort zone. By you beginning now, today, with very little effort, acting and behaving as though you were that key person you believe yourself to be, it is definitely an act of stepping out of your current fear and comfort zone that gives you great returns. If your dream or objective is to be an executive on your job, and you're currently a junior executive, what you're going to start doing is to start acting and behaving as though you already were that senior executive. This may include styling your hair a little differently, changing your wardrobe, or your attire. You're now starting to walk with more of a sense of urgency, importance, and confidence about yourself. You're going to start acting and behaving as though you already were that person you believe yourself to be, in this case that senior executive.

What I would like for you to do is to again go to your work manual, and what you're going to see there on page 5 is a blank list. There's where you will now write five to ten key things you can start effortlessly doing today, to commence your journey of "acting" as though you already were that person you believe yourself to be.

SO, DREAMERS, LET'S DO THIS NOW!

You have your list all written out. Some of the things that you have recorded there may appear relatively minute or small, but, believe it, or not it will definitely make a large and key difference in your life, if your emphasis is only put on a few of those smaller yet key areas on that list as far as you manifesting your dreams. For example, if your dream you have written down in your workbook in the earlier part of this workshop was that of purchasing a new car, one thing that we all know about that new car is that it's going to be shiny and clean. You can just smell the newness of it. Yet, the car that you're currently driving over time has become filthy and dirty, inside and out. This is really denoting you are not integrating your beliefs with your behavior. But this can be easily corrected. You see, the key thing you're going to do is you're going to go home after this workshop; you're going to clean that car up. You're going to make that car shiny and clean and smell good, just like that new car you're going to be driving. You're going to start living and integrating your dreams in to your life right now!

Again, let's say your dream is to purchase a new home, yet your apartment you're currently renting over time has become filthy, in need of paint, and has a dirty carpet, then you, again, are not living and integrating your dreams. The key thing you're going to have to do is this: You're going to have to, within your means right now, get your house in order! That house should be clean, smell good, just like that new house that you're going to be experiencing. This acting as though is a little invisible key that will give you much in life.

I'd like to share with you a personal story. A number of years ago, I would say back in 2002, I had a dream, a beautiful dream that I wanted to become an inspirational and a motivational speaker, because I just felt that I needed to and wanted to share with others the known roads I knew could make anyone's dreams become a realization in their lives. I always said to myself, if I had just had someone at an early stage or an early age in my life to help me and coach me and share with me this information that I'm now sharing with people, what a difference it would have made in my life.

I set out as my path, my dream, my objective of becoming an inspirational, motivational, and business speaker. One of the key things I found myself doing after I had seen this was a dream that had been enlightened to me is I joined Toastmasters International. Yes, it did help me tremendously, and I did receive my "CTM" designation as a "competent speaker." Although the substance of my speech was always there, I always felt I was failing over time in being able to present my presentations in a powerful and effective way that I knew was within me and that I was capable of. Despite all the skills that I had learned in Toastmasters, I just was not pulling it off, not until I literally stepped away from my physical world and actually started affirming and visually seeing myself mentally as the key speaker I wanted to be in my life. I would totally relax my entire head-to-toe body prior to falling to sleep at night, after which I would give verbal suggestions and affirmations to my subconscious mind. I "lulled" myself to sleep each night with this statement:" I am a dynamic speaker." I would also alternate this process with relaxing myself, prior to falling to sleep at night, and forming mental-imaged pictures of myself in my mind. I would picture in my mind I was on a platform and delivering the speech the way truly I wanted to. I would visualize my audience, the platform, and I would see myself walking back and forth across this platform as I delivered my speech to my audience. I would feel and see the gestures of my hands, my arms, and my facial expression as I related these powerful messages to my audience. Only then was I, during my waking hours, able to bring my dream to realization in my life.

Using these two key tools, "acting as though" and "mental visualization," as a means to bringing yours or anyone's dream into realization in your life are the true keys, for they can definitely over time give you more of what you want in life without you using more of nothing else in your life aside from your own mind and your faith in these sound and now discerned key principles. These two little things are what you can effortlessly start using tonight. You will be starting right where you are to shift the paradigms and beliefs about yourself to begin manifesting those dreams in your life. This acting as though and mental visualization are very important keys available to anyone to start utilizing now to aide them in vividly seeing their dream for themselves. There are numerous techniques and modalities available for anyone to utilize in their quest of seeing themselves as the person that they would like to be.

Note here that the tool you choose to use is one of personal preference, or free will. I share this with you to let you know that basically it doesn't matter what tool you use, as long as it is a positive and key tool you have observed works well for you over a short time period in aiding you in quickly quieting your mind to visualize any dream. Some tools that are available are imagery, as previously shown. This is where a person puts themselves in a semi-relaxed state, and they quiet their mind and picture themselves in their dreams, doing this on a daily basis. Also, try meditation, where you will utilize different mediums, such as the sound of running water from a fountain, burning candles, lying down in a quiet and semi-darkened room, or anything to help you quiet your mind.

By incorporating techniques such as mental visualization and imagery, along with acting "as though," you're effortlessly feeding and reprogramming your subconscious mind, the mind that's always under full control of your conscious mind in an effortless way or means of super-charging and, thereafter, turbo-boosting all your dreams into existence in your life.

GOOD LUCK, DREAMERS!

CHAPTER 10:
DREAM WORKSHOP: CONCLUSION

The workshop in this book you have just completed has been a three-part dream system, designed to be used in your life to accomplish your dreams and goals. This "Dream It First System" is available on CD at my website, www.dream-it-first.com, which includes beautiful music and a personal dream diary anyone can utilize as they follow the paths unfolded to them in this "Dream It First" program. This CD program has been designed to be listened to for a full thirty days, as it takes twenty-one days to form any new habit, yet it takes a full thirty days to reprogram the subconscious mind, which is, in essence, what you will be doing when you are replacing a smaller dream, or a nightmare, with a bigger dream in your life.

You see, as illustrated in the workshop just completed, the subconscious mind is a very powerful, yet beautiful and key tool to enable you to get anything that you want or desire in life, or to aide you in obtaining any dream that has been illuminated or enlightened to you with very little effort, whether that dream is getting out of debt, finding a soul mate, starting a business, seeking a spiritual life, or having increased health or fitness, whatever that dream is for you.

It is important to note that the word "subconscious" is derived from the word conscious, meaning the awareness of something. Your subconscious mind is subject to, and under full control of, your conscious mind. So with this truth you definitely have to guard what is thought about, seen, felt, and heard, and, yes, experienced over time in your conscious everyday awareness world, as it does, as previously shown, program the subconscious mind, which it is subject to and under full control of.

The subconscious mind is a mindless robot, whatever it is programmed with it will produce in your life. It does not tell you if the information you are programming it with is good or bad, or how to program it. It will only take orders impressed upon it. As has been denoted throughout this book thus far, you are simply being told to directly and indirectly "change your mind," which we now know feeds your subconscious mind, in order to change your world. That is the reason why it is imperative that you only want to have in your conscious awareness, that is, your conscious mind or your awareness, on a daily basis those positive thoughts and experiences.

This is simply done by monitoring the self-talk you give to yourself, as previously shown in the workshop. Monitor what you say to others, as well as the environments you place yourself in. Assess the mental food you tend to feed on by monitoring what goes into your mind on a daily basis. Monitor the negative people, the negative books that you read, the negative media that is seen on TV, and the negative information heard on your radio. Why? Because you now know that this negative stuff you have possibly been feeding and exposing yourself to over time has, without your awareness, been programming over time your subconscious mind, that mind that you do have full control over, if programmed correctly.

For it has automatically and involuntarily over the time in your life directed the non-manifesting or determent of your dreams in life. Yes, you, indeed, already have everything, regardless of how little it appears, that you need to manifest your dreams in life. Your only job in this workshop has been to effortlessly identify the key spiritual laws that have been unconsciously unfolded to you in this workshop, and begin today using them in your life today. Once your dreams or your desires have been enlightened to you, the only thing that will, thereafter, over time prevent you from ever making them a physical realization or manifestation in your life, is your thinking thereafter changed, which ultimately leads to your actions and dreams in your life. Yes, it is a beautiful thing to have your dreams given to you, and then effortlessly pioneered into existence by spiritual law, a force much greater than your conscious or physical world. Good luck, dreamers, as you have definitely done the preparation in this workshop for your enlightened dreams to effortlessly begin to manifest for you!

CHAPTER 11: DREAM ATTITUDE

A POEM

DREAM ATTITUDE

"As I travel through this life, over time the more I under-
    stand about life,

And the Dreams and Attitudes I must behold,

For they're more important than ostensible gold, or the past,

And present with all their entire toll,

Or the giftedness I may or may not behold.

For they have taken or made my scroll, my soul,

As well as your goals, so I am told, depending on my
    choices,

And how they were controlled.

The amazing thing is that I do have the choice

Of the Dreams and Attitudes I'll behold.

I cannot change the past, or the fact that unexpected
    changes will occur,

And the counters that others may avail to me each day.

For these are the sure foes that over time must unfold,
    which I indeed will have no control?

The things I do control are the Dreams and Attitudes I'll
    always behold,

They're the only key gold I truly do control."

By Jacqueline R. Robertson

Although we have just covered the three known roads to manifestation of our dreams and goals in the preceding workshops chapters, we are still ill-prepared in our quest to our enlightened dreams if we do not stop and look at the challenges in life that will inevitably occur, almost simultaneously, as we work towards our dreams and goals which have been enfolded to us.

This will be exactly what we will be looking at in this chapter, how we handle the unexpected changes that will inevitably occur over the time in our lives, without fail, en route to our enlightened dreams and goals in our life.

As mentioned throughout this book thus far, all of man's overall goals and dreams in life over time will basically be the same: achieving happiness, prosperity and health, in all areas, individually expressed by each of us. If this is the matter of all's concern, you may stop here, and wonder if, in fact, everyone's overall objective in life is basically the same, of simply having happiness, prosperity, and health, individually expressed in all areas of life. Why? Isn't everyone just "End-of-Story" happy and successful in their lives, and living their true dreams in life?

One of the many things which surely have over time prevented many people from obtaining and, thereafter, maintaining their enlightened dreams in life is their inability over time to weather all the storms, challenges, and the unexpected changes that will inevitably occur in their ever-changing lives. One's ability to weather these 80 percent or more elements, storms, and challenges over time in their lives is basically termed "Attitude," or their "Response" to life, what I refer to as simply having a "Dream Attitude" towards life. Having this key type of Attitude is basically having a focus driven and "belief-driven" attitude, this little key 20 percent more "response" towards and about life. Having this key 20 percent response, towards life is basically having an "I can" approach towards life, despite any unexpected changes, challenges, and storms, which may inevitably occur, without fail, en route to our goals and dreams in life. These negative, unexpected events are referred to as "nightmares," and they must and will over time occur in everyone's life.

No one person currently reading this book is exempt from these nightmares, storms, challenges, and unexpected changes over time occurring in their life. You're probably currently going through one in life right now, just finished with one, or getting ready to go through one. Definitely no one is exempt from nightmares and stuff happening in their life.

What we often refer to as "Stuff Just Happening" in our lives is basically the "changes" that will inevitably occur over time in our lives. One going through a job loss, bankruptcy, foreclosure, which is prevalent throughout the country right now, is just an unwanted "change." Anyone who has just lost a loved one or has experienced a divorce or breakup in a relationship has experienced an unwanted "change." Even our children over time no longer acting as though they have any sense is called a "change." Yes, all these nightmares that each and every one of us may experience are "unwanted changes" in our lives that we simply refer to as nightmares, and "stuff happening" in our lives.

It's very easy to weather the good stuff that occurs over time in our lives with a positive, pro-active, winning "Dream Attitude," but it's definitely more of a challenge to weather the negative stuff with this pro-active "I Can Dream Attitude." It surely is a challenge to weather all the unexpected changes in our lives, yet maintain a positive attitude of focus on our enlightened dreams. While we're on the subject of "changes" in our lives, I'd like to give you a brief history about this thing called "change," so you know where I'm coming from. Before I do this, I'm going to have to take a fairly strong position here by letting you know, if you do not already, that I do believe in "creation."

I believe when God initially created Man, he did create him (100 percent) "perfect." Perfect means that changes don't occur! We over time don't grow old, we do not experience sickness or pain (physically or mentally); we don't even die. Yet, we all know the little story of our little "Brother and Sister" Adam and Eve. They sort of messed up! They made a big mistake! Well, as a result of this big key mistake, or "cause," we were over time to experience the "effects" and" "affect" of "changes" over time in our lives. Yes, over time we will certainly grow old, we will all also over time in our lives experience sickness and pain, physically as well as mentally in our lives.

So if this thing called "change" or "changes" or the "time" in which these changes were to occur was not our Creator's initial intention or goal for us over the time in our lives, then one may easily postulate that this thing called "change," as well as the time periods in which it occurs has to be "humanly abnormal," so it must also follow that if "change" and the time in which it occurs is "abnormal," then our reactions in life over time to this thing called "change," as well as to "time," must be "normal." I want you to never doubt that your initial reactions to the "negative stuff" and "unwanted changes" (that we call "nightmares") and the time in which they occur in our lives (over time) are abnormal, or wrong in any way. It is definitely normal.

If you were cooking on your stove and accidentally burned yourself, your normal reaction to this painful stimulus, or unwanted change, would be to immediately holler and pull your arm away, or pull your arm away and holler. I'm not sure what order this would occur in, but this is a "normal" reaction, isn't it? But are you going to stand there over time, and holler, and pull your arm away for the next twenty-four hours, or are you going to get to "responding" with whatever you have available to you? Yes! I think you're going to possibly ice that wound, apply a little antibiotic to that wound, then possibly wrap that wound, and then move on.

This is what you're going to have to do with the storms, challenges, setbacks, defeats, nightmares, and unexpected changes that occur over time in your life. Go ahead and react initially if you have to. It's "normal." React if you must. But hopefully, it's not too long over time, and when you get through with this "normal reaction," over a short or either long period of time in your life you're going to have to get to a little 20 percent effort called "responding" and get back to your dreams in life.

You see, it's not what happens over time to you in life, because stuff will always happen over time in our lives. Yet, it's how you "respond" over that time to the stuff that happens to you in your life that makes the difference. You see, when you react to stuff that happens over time to you in your life, you allow that thing over time to take away your dream. You allow that thing over time to take away your peace. You allow that thing over time to take away your happiness. You allow that thing over the time in your life to take away precious moments, minutes, hours, days, and years away from your life.

When you "respond" to the stuff that happens to you over time, you take your life back. You're in control, and then able to get back to your dreams in life. This little thing called "responding," over time which is our key attitudes towards life, is big, big business, for it will definitely over time make or break your dreams in life, for it is the little thing that gives us much in life.

Have you ever encountered someone in your life, someone you may personally know right now in your life that's experienced tremendous setbacks, challenges, and defeats, and unexpected changes continuously in their life over time? But they were able over short periods of time to get back on track to get back to their dreams? On the other hand, have you ever encountered someone you know possibly right now in your life that has experienced these same tremendous setbacks, defeats, and changes over time, but they were never quite able over time to get back on track and get back to their dreams in life? They got kind of caught up over time in the "reaction."

I know, at this point, many of you may be seriously pondering this next question: How does one maintain this so-called positive "Dream Attitude" over time when they're going through all this stuff and unexpected negative changes in their lives that appear to be taking them directly away from their dreams in life? Stuff like losing their job, people mistreating them, having financial and relationship problems. Believe it or not, the number one key thing that's going to help you weather these unexpected storms and challenges in your life over time is your "mind," which produces your thoughts. Yes, those positive thoughts you use to communicate to yourself day in and day out is the only 20 percent more effort that you can use to counter these nightmares, storms, challenges, and unexpected change in your life.

It's important to share with you at this point an important psychological truth about your key thoughts. They, in fact, will dictate all of your key feelings and your key emotions and those feelings and your emotions are what will lead to your key actions in life. A lot of these key actions may not always be consistent with your key dreams. This is what we see many times happening over time with a lot of our youth today, where their feelings and their emotions contribute to their actions, sometimes without them even being aware of it. Such actions, like dropping out of school, promiscuous sex, or even the use of drugs initially stem from their thoughts they communicate to themselves day in and day out when they were going through the midst of unexpected and unwanted changes in their lives.

We all will definitely choose our life. That is, we do choose all the conditions of our life over time when we choose the thoughts we over time allow our mind to dwell on. You cannot have one type of mindset over time and another different type of external world over time around us, nor can we simply have one type of external world over time, and another totally different type of mindset over time. This means that you cannot change over time your external world for the better and not leave your mind unchanged over time for the better, nor can you simply change your mind for the better and not over time change your external world for the better. In other words, when you change your mind, again, you change your whole world, your whole life. With this in mind, the only 20 percent more effort, which is the 20 percent key needed, is to definitely work on changing your "mind," and as a result of doing this little 20 percent more effort, you are definitely changing your external world and your own conditions in life. Yes, your thoughts, which stem from your mind, are a very profound and powerful tool for you to start using today in developing over a short time those dreams which have been enlightened to you.

To further illustrate this point, I would like to share with you the following unfortunate story. Some years ago I had two very unfortunate opportunities to speak at two separate funeral services of two family members who had sadly committed suicide at a relatively young age. What do you think over time led both of these young men to their unfortunate acts that suddenly ended their lives? Believe it or not, it all started with their own "mind," which elicited their thinking process or thoughts. Yes, apparently negative thoughts they communicated to themselves day in and day out as they were going through their unexpected changes, pain and storms in their lives were to blame.

They most likely found themselves focusing over time on thoughts of loneliness, thoughts of bewilderedness, thoughts of despair, and thoughts of hopelessness, and yes, apparently negative thoughts about death. These thoughts in turn over time transcended into their emotions and their feelings, which over time led to their actions, those negative actions that ceased all their dreams they may have had in their lives.

What I'm getting ready to say may sound quite insignificant, yet it is a very key and profound statement. Did you know "just a change in these two men's mind" over time is all that they really needed. This "change in their minds" over time would have, believe it or not, taken them both (over time) in totally different key directions, and they would be here with us today. I share this very unfortunate story with you to show just how crucial it is we learn to perform this little 20 percent more effort of communicating only positive thoughts to ourselves, especially when we're walking through our pain, storms, nightmares, and unexpected changes in life.

If you just got word on your job they were down-sizing, and there were going to be some tremendous layoffs in the next coming months, an initial "normal" reaction to this negative change or this bad news in your thinking may be "Oh, my God, I don't know what I'm going to do! I can hardly pay my bills as it is! We're going to lose the house!" Let's take a look at what happens from this point on. From the moment you manifest those "nightmares" in your thinking, what you've done is you've set up, yes, that key "Law of Attraction" to attract over time what you don't want, yet you're consciously staying focused on to attract and manifest in your life. Those things over time will definitely happen if those thoughts are not immediately countered or replaced with positive self-talk. Why? Because this key negative self-talk that you find yourself giving and programming your subconscious mind with will, in approximately twenty to twenty-one days, become your habit. As a result of this bad habit, you will keep on over time giving yourself this negative information. You'll keep on working on it, and the things that you're communicating to yourself, those negative thoughts, will definitely seek into your subconscious mind to work to bring those nightmares to pass or in existence in your life.

A positive response to this same news would be "Hmm, that's interesting. I know I'm not going out like that. I better get busy! That resume that I've been procrastinating on for the past year or so, I think I better go ahead and get it finished. Possibly that job that John, my co-worker, was just telling me about a couple of weeks ago, which I thought I didn't want, I think I'll go ahead and 'check it out.' I'm going to subscribe to the Sunday Times today, so I can see what's going on in the workplace, and where I now can best utilize my acquired skills."

From the moment you have consciously manifested those positive thoughts, you have again set into motion the powerful "law of attraction" to begin attracting over time that which you want, and have stayed focused on, in your life. Why? Because you're going to keep on performing this positive habit, and all the positive info you're communicating to yourself will then seek into your subconscious mind to attract over time your dreams into your life. Although you won't know how or when those dreams will happen, they will definitely happen in your life, despite the unexpected stuff and changes that have occurred.

Again, it's very imperative you learn to communicate only positive thoughts and right thinking, which will over time produce right action, to yourself in the midst of any storms, challenges, and unexpected changes that occur in your life. I'm going to introduce you to someone, which you can use over time as a key mental tool to help you stay focused and maintain this needed positive "Dream Attitude" in life. His name is "Mr. Attitude," and for you guys reading this book, you can refer to this person as "Miss Attitude."

All the nightmares, storms, unexpected changes, and challenges you find yourself going through over time in life, and you're telling yourself, as well as others, negative information, such as "I can't do it," "It's not working for me," and all the other garbage you may find you're telling yourself, Mr. or Miss Attitude, (this key invisible person) are going to poke you in the neck and they're going to have you immediately replace that negative garbage with positive self-talk.

Mr. or Miss Attitude is going to tell you, "Yes!" "You can," "You can do this," "You're no longer susceptible to those old lies, myths, and beliefs about yourself." Mr. or Mrs. Attitude is going to poke you in your neck every time you use negative self-talk. They're going to tell you, "No! You're not going to give up. You're going to keep on walking right through this nightmare."

Believe me, many of you are going to over time have a lot of pokes and bruises in your neck, and I am not sure how you're going to explain this to a lot of people in your life, but that's okay! Because it's definitely over any time okay for you to say to yourself, "I can. I will." Yes, there are go-ing to be a lot of key things and situations over time in life you don't have control over, but as quoted in the "Serenity Prayer" many use to overcome addictions in life, "You are going to have to have the wisdom to accept the (key) things that you cannot change, and have within you the power to change the (key) things you can change." The one key thing you can change over time that you do have absolute power over is your "mind," which in turn will produce your attitude and your responses in life and over time lead to your dreams. That's the one thing you can change.

Just know this is the one thing no one over any time in your life can ever take away from you. They *cannot* take away the thoughts that stem from your "mind." Your thoughts, and the thereafter words you use and speak over your life, are the tools that are going to help you weather any and every peril that will undoubtedly occur over time in your life. Yes, this thing called "Dream Attitude" may be the little minute thing many over time have taken lightly, yet it over time does deliver grand results with its use. This is definitely a little 20 percent effort that gives anyone much in their lives. If anyone in life wishes to have a different end result over time in their lives, different than what they're currently experiencing, they're definitely going to have to start doing things differently start-ing today. If anyone chooses to have or maintain a negative, doubtful attitude, and they continue to maintain this type of attitude over time, yet simultaneously wonder why things aren't happening for them, it may be time for them to simply "change their minds," which will surely over time change their world and lead them to their dreams in life. We all may be aware of Albert Einstein's definition of "insanity," which means "Doing the same thing over and over and expecting a different result, yet getting the same result." Yet, there does appear to be a 20 percent group in life who do not fit this overt definition, because they know the one effortless thing they can do more of in their life is to maintain a positive, pro-active "I Can Dream Attitude" towards life, despite any "nightmares" they have or will experience in life. This they know is the little 20 percent more key effort that will lead them over time to any of their greater dreams in life every time, without fail.

Many times people have asked me this question time and time again, "Jacqueline, just how have you over time been able to weather so many storms in life, yet stay focused on manifesting your enlightened dreams?" Sometimes, the only little small thing I could tell them was "Over time I just kept on walking, and kept on talking." You see, every storm has a beginning, and every storm over time has its own ending. If you just keep on walking and keep on talking "positively" to yourself through those storms, you're eventually over time walk yourself right through every single storm in your life. Your key ability to keep walking and keep talking positively to yourself is termed 'attitude,' and this key thing called 'Dream Attitude,' given to me by God over time, has indeed been my true key!"

WHAT IF?

CHAPTER 12: THE LAW OF SACRIFICE AND UNIFICATION:

I have chosen to call the subtitle of this concise chapter "What If?" to candidly communicate to those reading this book that if they find themselves, as well as others, using this statement en route to their enlightened dreams in life, then this is surely a key red flag or signal that should indicate they have <u>not over time</u> built the needed mental, emotional, or spiritual equivalent for their enlightened dreams in life, as shown in chapter 4. This will, as also shown in the same chapter, will surely prevent their dreams from ever becoming "Dry Land," keeping their enlightened "dreams" in life in the "want" category. Why? Simply because their ostensible dream(s) actually aren't dreams at all, just merely "wants" they have.

The statement "What If?" implies in anyone's thoughts or thinking process negativity, or "Lack and Limitation," about their dreams. Again, as shown earlier in Chapter 3, this "Lack and Limitation," which may occur in many people's thinking is really called "fear," the fear there may be a loss of something or there's not enough of something.

The true acronym for the word "fear" as shown on the following page is "False events appearing real." This will always, without fail, prevent many people's dreams over time in their lives from ever becoming firm "Dry Land." Depicted in the following page is the true acronym for the word "Faith," which is "False appearances into turned hope." This is what will always counter any fears in life.

80/20 DREAM FORMULA EQUATION

FEAR IS:

False

Events

Appearing

Real

Fear subtracted from Faith equals an 80 percent or more Manifestation.

⇧   ⇧

100%   –   20% = 80% Manifestation

FAITH IS:

False

Appearances

Into

Turned

Hope

Faith subtracted from Fear equals an 80 percent or more Manifestation.

⇧   ⇧

20%   –   100% = 80% Manifestation

Faith is the substance of things hoped for and the evident (events) of things not seen, and

Fear is the substance of things that appear "real," yet are not.

"CHOOSE TODAY WHO YOU WILL SERVE—FAITH OR FEAR!"

As I over time begin to have a fuller understanding of the above equation, as it pertained to all dreams in life, I would give public talks on the topic of "perseverance." One of the major facets I would share with my audience was a person who perseveres in anything must also be "committed." I would relate, to my audiences, the importance of commitment towards any dream in life, and what it took to be "committed" to any dream in life. It would follow, in these talks, if one is committed they are actually "willing" to do whatever it takes, and they could not possibly be saying, simultaneously, these statements "What if this or that happens?" These things, although they are possibilities, or may appear to be probable events, they in actuality cannot be thought or even spoken about. They cannot be dwelled upon at all. How can they be, and not keep anyone in an ambivalent state, without action towards their dreams in life?

This is where the beautiful spiritual law of "sacrifice and unification" comes into play. This law of "sacrifice and unification" is a beautiful law few (maybe only approximately 20 percent or less of the population) have discerned or have fully understood. Yet, if this law is understood, and thereafter implemented, it can bring overwhelming benefits. This law of "sacrifice and unification" states if one is asked to give up something, and that "something" is "real," it will over time come back to them. Note here the word "real." It is of great importance.

In the Bible, Abraham was asked by God to sacrifice his most precious key possession. That most precious key possession, in Abraham's case, was his son Isaac. His son, Isaac, was something that was precious to Abraham, which he greatly adored. This sacrifice, if made by him, would have indeed been one of his most precious possessions he beheld. This sacrifice requested of him, to say the least, must have been a painstaking request, and definitely an unwanted desire. But Abraham, being subservient and under full submission to his dream of serving God, gave up his most adorned key possession, his son. Yet, the key flip side of this law, which is also very important, indicates, as I noted earlier, if the thing or sacrifice you are asked to be given up is "real," then that thing or sacrifice given up will effortlessly over time come back to you. In the case of Abraham, the "thing" or sacrifice he was asked to give up was his son, because his son was "real." If you know the story, Abraham did not have to give up his son after all, and he was over time effortlessly reunited with him.

The point here is Abraham was simply "willing," that is, he was totally committed to his dream of apparently serving God, and he was willing to do whatever it took, even though it meant being willing to give up his most precious possession, his son. His "willingness" was the only 20 percent key and effort needed; he did not have to sacrifice his son, yet had to be "willing."

You see, the word "willing" is the key 20 percent. It denotes total commitment. In actuality, many times you will not have to give up your most precious possessions, if they are real, yet you must be willing. Your unwillingness, believe it or not, is what's keeping you from going forth. It's important to note here one's unwillingness is really centered on or around fear. This is what makes it difficult to give up something, not the actual sacrifice itself. Somewhere hidden in the equations we are saying, "What if this or that" occurs, which again simply denotes our fear.

This brings to mind something my secretary (at that time), Adrie, had said to me awhile back when I was struggling with a key personal dilemma, a very difficult choice I had been faced with making in my life. She said to me in her quiet, sweet, meek voice, "If you love someone so much and you're willing to give him up, if he comes back to you, over time he's yours." I remember this touching me deeply. In my case I did risk giving up my special person in my life, and since he was "real," he over time came back to me.

You see, many times in quests, and en route to our true dreams, we may be asked to give up something, or even someone that is very, or apparently very, precious to us, which is, in fact, often the block or the kingpin deterring or preventing us from going forward in our lives, and having a unification with our dreams and goals in our life, that is, if we are not physically "willing" or even mentally willing to say we will release it. In many cases, the thing we are most unwilling to say we will give up or sacrifice is the very thing (or the fear) we need to give up or let go of in order to move forward towards our dreams in life. This is surely very hard for many to do when they're simply leading and leaning on their own understanding, and not the understanding of spiritual law. I now see this "unwillingness" is what caused me much pain in my life, and subsequently caused me to endure a needless long, six-year divorce battle of extreme pain, as spoken about earlier, simply because I was, at that time, "unwilling" to give up, due to fear, those things which apparently appeared real, but in actually were not, which delayed and could have permanently over time prevented me from manifesting bigger dreams in life.

As you recall earlier, this law says if that key thing you are called to give up is real, it will definitely come back to you. If it does not come back, what you have done, in actuality, is made room for a bigger key thing or something bigger and grander in its place, for any space already occupied cannot be occupied by something else already there. Two things cannot occupy the same space at the same time. An example of this law in effect is as follows: If you want a new sofa in your living room, because the one you now have is beat-up and worn, you must get rid of that old sofa before it can be replaced with a new one, as two objects cannot occupy the same space. You must have the faith and belief a new sofa will soon take that old sofa's place. In essence, you must be willing to sacrifice that old sofa, of a lesser value, for something new and of a greater value. So get rid of that sofa! Or anything else blocking your dreams. Make room for the new key thing that's on its way! This law of "sacrifice and unification" is indeed a powerful and beautiful key law.

This law is one of utmost importance to incorporate, or to have an awareness of, once any dream or dreams have been enlightened to you, for one must know in order to have growth, one indeed has to risk (false or unreal) security.

This brings to mind the beautiful story of Chris Gardner, a book later made into a motion picture starring Will Smith. This man was faced over time with giving up, sacrificing his apparent security, his home, his wife, and all his other worldly possessions in quest of his enlightened dreams in his life. He found himself homeless and living on the street with his small son. He was faced with giving up all the things that appeared "real" in his life, yet they were not "real," only "false security" that appeared real. They were indeed replaced over time with real and grander "real" dreams he had for himself in his life. Those things that were real he did retain. In this case, he, too, was able. Of all the things he gave up, he was able to retain his son. That was "real," along with other beautiful dreams of health, prosperity, and great abundance that had been enlightened to him. This is indeed a beautiful story to show the beautiful law of "sacrifice and unification" in action.

CHAPTER 13: THE RECIPROCITY PATH
THE LAW OF RECIPROCITY

Before we bring closure to this book, "Dream It First, The 80/20% (Spiritual) Laws to Manifestation of Your Goals and Dreams," we cannot do so without examining the spiritual law and seed of "reciprocity," which is the law of "giving and receiving" in quests of one's enlightened dreams in life. Although the spiritual laws unfolded to you in this book thus far are in themselves sufficient in providing the paths to manifestation of your dreams in life, if one is to add overwhelming increased abundance to their dreams as written in the Bible, "press down" and "shaken together," then this law must be fully isolated, identified, understood, and then used in order to derive the full benefits of its beautiful working properties.

So, dreamers, let's begin! The word "reciprocity" stems from the word "reciprocal," meaning "one, then the other." It is the spiritual law of "giving and receiving." I will examine here with you the inner working components of this beautiful law.

If one would simply look at the words "giving and receiving" or the words "receiving and giving," and view it as one whole entity, or these two separate words combined together as one whole word, one could clearly see one cannot have one (giving) without the other word (receiving) reciprocating. This is what makes these two words "a whole" working unit, as seen here in the following sentence: As one gives willingly of himself over time with the resources that he or she has to another, who in turn is then willingly receiving it over time, he is in actuality over time giving back to himself, because he is part of that whole. This is spiritual law. You may have already discovered thus far in this book the true definition of the word "law" simply means "how something works." Now you see and understand why we cannot simply only want to give to another; we must give in order for this law to work. I'm sure most of us are all indeed giving 100 percent effort of what we think we should do in our lives to add increased abundance to ourselves, yet if we would implement this law, as shown and depicted above, we would then no longer lean on our own previous understanding, but would, in fact, simply act only in accordance with how this law works, by an increased 20 percent more (willing) giving of whatever resources that we do currently have Such as time, knowledge, wisdom, service, money, or whatever is an added surplus or resource for us.

The Bible states, "That when much is given, much is expected." What this is saying is: if much of something is given to one in a particular area over time in their life in terms of time, knowledge, wisdom, or even money, then much of that, or even greater, is expected to be given. I know many of you may counter this latter statement with "I don't have a surplus of anything to give. I'm just barely making ends meet, and I don't have one single surplus of anything to give." Yet, this is not factually true, because everyone, including you, indeed has been given over time a surplus or resource of something others do not have or possess. This surplus is not always money, which most think it should be. That's why we see a myriad of people giving in a myriad of different ways. For these areas they give from are simply their surplus or resource that has been given to them in different areas in their life. As you look at these happy "givers" in life over time, you may also see and observe one common thing they all seem to share, which is, although they give in abundance, their storehouse in which they give from, whether it is money, time, knowledge, or wisdom, is never dry or depleted. This is regardless of what goes on economically in the world, or whatever economic season or "changes" that occurs.

This is why it's said "Do what you love and the money over time will come," for when you're doing what you love, whether you're making money at it or not, you're usually happy in that endeavor. This happiness is what attracts your abundance, which is the "law of attraction" again in actions. This is why it's very important not to give from their "storehouse" or your resources, if you're not happy in your giving. Why? Because in your giving you cannot achieve, nor benefit from, the fullness of this law. Let me explain why. When one gives with a happy heart, they're in essence giving with love. It's important to note here the word "love" is synonymous with the words "the law of attraction," for love (for something good or even bad) is what sets up this law, and why it is said it is synonymous, meaning the same. When you're happy as a result of doing something good which you love, you simultaneously set up the law of attraction to attract back to you over time those same good things which you have given, increased, "press down" in abundance, although your abundance will not usually flow from the source or persons you have given to.

This may account for the reason you see people giving in some areas and not in others, yet never over time expecting anything from those which they given to, because they are giving according to their heart's condition. If that condition is of willingness, goodness, and that of love and of happiness, and they in turn give from this state, they're setting up this law for what was given to be attracted over time back to them. What they know is that if they give from their storehouse and it's not from positive willingness, love and happiness, this law cannot, or will not, work for them.

It is important to note one should not feel under any duress, or undue influence, or guilt in their giving, for we are definitely aware of our storehouse, whether we admit it or not, and we are definitely aware of our surpluses and our individual resources. The storehouse may consist of money, the storehouse may consist of time, the storehouse may consist of knowledge, the storehouse may consist of wisdom, and the storehouse may also consist of what is called "service." Since giving and receiving is truly one working unit, as shown earlier, it is important the one who is on the receiving end willingly accepts what is given to them with gratitude, not feeling obligated to reciprocate. If they do reciprocate over time, it, too, must be given over time from their own "personal storehouse," which may or may not be the same as the giver's "storehouse." It, too, must be given positively and willingly with love from a surplus they have, which denotes that no "force" of any nature should be used, as shown earlier, or is needed.

Many of us are abreast, or are totally aware of what is meant by the surplus of money. Maybe, we understand the surplus of time, knowledge, wisdom, and talent, but many have not fully discerned their storehouse of "service." This one key resource is one we all are endowed with, if you have no other surplus to give from. Yet, this little 20 percent resource we all are endowed with has not always been fully identified as that.

Yes, we are all going to have to be able to render over time some type of key "service" in order to get to this thing called "our dreams" in life. This is regardless of what role you hold or play in life. This service you must render over time has nothing to do with your job title, or whether it's a prestigious title or not. Why? Because we're all in the "service business," regardless of our key roles in life. This means we are all basically a "servant" in our daily endeavors. If you're a doctor, a therapist, a nurse, or any other allied healthcare professional, you deliver a service to your patients.

If you're a broker, attorney, accountant, or self-employed, you deliver service to your clients. If you're a truck driver, a waitress, or a custodian, you deliver service to your customers. If you're a parishioner in a church, you deliver a service to that church and to God. If you're a politician, you deliver service to your constituents. If you are a mother or father, a husband or wife, you, too, deliver a service to your spouse and to your children. Why? Simply because we are all in this "key business of serving," what this is really saying we are all basically "servants." Yet, even with this knowledge, did you know approximately 80 percent or more of the population in the world doesn't want to be labeled as being any

type of "servant"? They really don't want their job descrip-
tion, their role in life, or anything having to do with them
to be associated with anything that has to do with serving
someone else. Why is this? Simply because approximately
80 percent or more of the population sees a servant as being
someone that's less than, or inferior. But if you would take
the time to look up this little 20 percent effort in your dictionary, the word "service" would be simply defined as a big
80 percent or better value of being "an assistance or benefit
to another." This really puts a "servant" in a key superior 80
percent or better position, as opposed to an inferior 20 percent or lesser position, because they're providing a (greater
80 percent) "assistance" or greater value to another.

If you would read further regarding this same definition,
in that same dictionary, you would see that it also has a two-
fold or dual definition, as being "the manner in which you're
waited on," simply meaning "the manner in which you're
served." We see this on countless of occasions when we dine
in a restaurant. Sometimes, the "manner" in which you're
waited on or the manner in which you were served by that
waiter or waitress makes you feel a little bit unserved. To
further illustrate this, you may have heard that "It's not what
you say that matters, but how it's said." We also see this on
countless of occasions in the breakdown of a family unit.
One family member feels and believes he or she is "giving"
love and service, but the one "receiving" it doesn't really
perceive it that way, simply because of the manner in which
the "service" is given. It's very important to note the way the
person who's "receiving" that service over time "perceives"
that service from the "giver," as shown in Chapter 6, is what
makes it real to them, or makes it more important than the
actual service itself.

If you were out on your patio grilling some delicious T-
bone steaks, and your little dog came up to you because he
smelled the aroma of those steaks, sat there on his little hind
legs, and began to beg for a piece of meat, you, wanting to
be of service to him, would then cut a small slice of that

meat and toss it to him. Indeed, he would perceive this delivery as "service," and he would be very happy. What if a family member came out and asked you for a piece of that same meat, and you followed the same procedure you used when you delivered the piece of meat to the dog, you simply cut a slice of that meat and tossed it to them? Indeed, that family member would not be very happy, nor would he perceive this delivery as any type service at all. I can't really tell you what course of events would have occurred after that!

You see, service for humans is service that must be rendered or delivered over time with a little 20 percent effort called quality or what's referred to as "integrity," yet it seems approximately 80 percent or more of the population really doesn't know the true meaning of the word "integrity." They may use the word, or hear the word being used, yet they have never really known its full meaning. If you would take the time to look up this word in your dictionary, it would simply be defined as "complete, unbroken." This really says little, yet it implies much, a real 80/20 rule in effect, for service rendered or delivered with "integrity" is service rendered or delivered "over time" with truthfulness, honesty, thankfulness, loyalty, and with love, complete and unbroken. It's synonymous with the word "fidelity," meaning the faithfulness in the discharge of a duty, the same fidelity expected in a marriage relationship. It's further defined as a "quality or state of being faithful," a "quality of reproduction," which equates to the reproduction of "love," which we now know from the previous chapters sets up the "law of attraction" to begin working in our lives.

You see, if you're not rendering or delivering quality service with faithfulness, honesty, truthfulness, loyalty, complete and unbroken, which equates to love and a state of "happiness," you're basically not delivering or rendering service at all. The person receiving that service over time will definitely know this and will not perceive it as service, which makes it impossible for this "law of reciprocity" of "giving and receiving" to work in your life.

In an interview being given by the late Johnnie Cochran, a prominent civil rights attorney, he was asked, "Just how have you been able to achieve all your success and happiness in life?" I recall his profound response touching me deeply. His response was "Service is the rent that I pay for the space that I occupy in life." What a beautiful expression to represent the benefits of rendering service over time with quality, integrity, and love. After pondering this statement for some time, it later came to my awareness this same powerful phrase was originally coined by the late Dr. Martin Luther King. For service over the time in his life was indeed the rent he had paid for the space he occupied, and still occupies in many people lives today. When I took this statement and began to examine it from a personal perspective, I was indeed astounded, for I clearly began to see this thing called "service" has over time been the rent I, too, have paid for the space I occupy in life.

I begin to clearly see that this thing called "service" is what has given me happiness from all the people I have served over the time in my life. This thing called "service" is what has indirectly given me the beautiful, mortgage-free home I live in, the nice cars I drive, nice clothes I wear, and all the other finer amenities I happily benefit from in life. These things, indeed over time, have been my return on and of my effortless investment of "service."

So if you're possibly wondering today how you have or have not achieved over time the space, the dreams, and goals that you would like to occupy in life, you may need to assess the key service, not some of the services, but all the key services you're rendering and delivering to people in your life, en route to your dreams in life. Simply ask yourself this question: "Have I over time been rendering service with quality, faithfulness, honesty, truthfulness, loyalty, complete and unbroken, which all equates to "love." If you are delivering services with these key fine qualities, then happiness, prosperity, and great abundance are definitely inevitable for you.

CHAPTER 14: THE LAW OF CAUSE AND EFFECT

The "law of cause and effect" is one of the greatest of all laws. Not only spiritual law, it is the heart of all cosmic laws, including the laws of mathematics, chemistry, and physics. In accordance it is the cosmic law of all laws presented to you in this book. All the laws that have been presented to you are incorporated within this one law, the "law of cause and effect," which implies for every action in life over time there is a reaction, A "reaction" which gives you more of what you want in life, or less of the same.

Hence, the "action" is the" cause" and the "reaction" is the" effect." As we have seen in this book, the 20 percent action is the cause for the 80 percent reaction, or the 80 percent reaction is caused by the 20 percent action. To be put another way, the 20 percent cause gives us the 80 percent effects, or the 80 percent effects are caused by a 20 percent cause. If this is an arduous task for you to comprehend or understand, you may choose to look and interpret it the following way: "For every action in life, there is over time a positive or negative reaction, or end result." This law is applicable to all, I mean all, aspects of life. With your basic understanding of this law as presented here, you must know, discern, and recognize here you are, or have over time been, the "cause" for your entire positive or negative 80 percent or 20 percent effects or results you have obtained in life.

This may be difficult to comprehend, or maybe postulate, when you do not view or perceive things in this way. If you are blaming, that is, putting the "effects"(results) outside of yourself, and putting the effects (results) on others, which are people and events, you will not or cannot perceive or understand the way this law works. As a result of this, you will not be able to use this law in obtaining and, thereafter, maintaining your key dreams in life.

When you can understand no one cause outside of yourself over time has been the cause for where you are in life right now, or where you have been in the past, you may indeed want to just simply close this book at once. With the knowledge of this possible occurrence, I have indeed saved this short chapter for last. If you choose to not continue, it will be definitely okay to close this book at this point, and read no further. Yes, you are the key "cause" for every, I mean, every effect or thing that is happening or has happened to you over time in your life, no one else.

If one does not like the way their life, or dreams in life, is currently going, they must then know if they are the cause, as previously denoted above, then it should follow the effects can then over time be changed simply by changing the cause, which is, themselves. I shared in one of the previous chapters the old cliché: If you keep doing the same thing over and over again over time in life, expecting a different result, but getting the same result, that's termed "insanity." With this in mind if one wishes to stop any key "insanity" in their lives right now, they in truth would need to change the cause, which is to change themselves and their actions. This is what I painstakingly over time learned from my "insane" six-year chronic divorce. Once I stopped and let go of the cause (which I was unconsciously producing by my thoughts and only focus being on all the key things I was loosing that I thought were "real," yet were not), all the effects then stopped. I was then able to move forth with my dreams in life, one of which is this book you're now reading.

One needs to simply, as implied throughout this book, "change their key or mind" and hence change their world, which are all the effects they are getting. Yes, throughout this book you have been instructed subliminally, if not directly, to change the "cause," that is yourself, in order to derive at a different key end result, which are your dreams in life. When we change our key or "mind," We're changing the thoughts we allow to enter our mind.

When one "changes their mind," they in fact let go of old key beliefs, old key belief systems, and key paradigms not of service to them in their quest of reaching and maintaining their key enlightened dreams in life. These old beliefs have subconsciously, as we spoke about in the previous chapters, driven and indirectly directed their lives, yet have not over time provided them with what they truly wish, or want, in terms of their dreams in life.

As discussed in the previous chapter, when one changes their "thoughts" that stem from their mind to that of key "right thinking," or what's referred to as key "right consciousness," or what some will refer to as "key action," what they have actually done is over time changed the "cause" that will definitely change the effects in their world. When we, on a daily basis, incorporate fear, doubt, blame, unhappiness, sadness, worry, anxiety, envy, resentment, fighting, or any other negative thought or action, we are then communicating these negative "causes" to ourselves, hence our lives. As discussed in the previous chapters, we now know these things are really the "cause" for our "effects" we have in our lives. That is why it is important to rid these "causes" and replace them with better "causes" that will yield better effects in our lives. Yes, we indeed must rid these negative effects in our lives with causes that will deliver better effects, which are our enlightened dreams in life. This must happen regardless of what's going on in the exterior world around us, which we perceive through our key five senses, for these senses, which we all perceive our external world through, may indeed "cause" us to say "no" about our dreams. Yet, you must, as we used to say in the "old school days," "psyche yourself out," going within yourself, because it's definitely okay to live in a key "fantasy world," "causing" the better "effects" over time to occur in your lives, which are your enlightened dreams.

Chapter 15: <u>Your Workshop Manual</u>
<u>&</u>
<u>Dream Diary</u>

DREAM WORKSHOP
MANUAL/DIARY

Write down events or circumstances which you feel have led you to any present nightmare:

1. _____

_____

2. _____

_____

3. _____

_____

4. _____

_____

5. _____

_____

DREAM PHOTOGRAPHING
Your photograph must be written using the 3 "Ps."

1. Present Tense
2. Personal
3. Positive

Your photograph must also be written in full detail
Write out your dream using these above 3 "Ps" and in detailed form.

1. _____

_____

2. _____

_____

3. _____

_____

REPLACING NEGATIVE SELF TALK

NEGATIVE DREAM TALK	REPLACE WITH POSITIVE DREAM TALK
1. I can't	1.
2. I don't know how	2.
3. My health is poor	3.
4. I'm too fat	4.
5. I'll try	5.
6. I'm so stupid	6.
7. I can't afford it	7.
8. I'll do it later	8.
9. It's not my fault	9.
10. I have no choice	10.
11. It's not working out	11.
12. It's too hard	12.
13. I'm too poor	13.
14. I'm too tried	14.
15. I'm not smart enough	15.
16. I don't have the time	16.
17. I don't have money	17.
18. What if it doesn't work out?	18.
19. I don't know how it will work out	19.
20. I don't know the right people	20.
21. I'm not good at this	21.
22. What if I lose my money?	22.

ACTING OUT YOUR DREAMS
Ways I can start behaving as though I'm already the key person I dream/believe myself to be.
Today I will:

1. Start: _____

2. Start: _____

3. Start: _____

4. Start: _____

5. Start: _____

6. Start: _____

7. Start: _____

8. Start: _____

9. Start: _____

10. Start: _____

11. Start:: _____

12. Start:: _____

MY DREAM DIARY NOTES

_____

_____

_____

_____

_____

_____

_____

_____

_____

_____

CHAPTER 16

The conclusion of this book has come about over time in a strange, yet, uncanny, definite way, as I had for sometime, throughout the writing of this book, often wondered how I could conclude this book, yet simultaneously stream together all of these beautiful spiritual laws, conveyed in this book, into a near perfect whole. Although consciously this appeared to be a challenging and somewhat arduous undertaking, I found myself letting go of these thoughts in order not to impede my thinking process and my quest of completing this book. Shortly after the book was, in fact, 80 percent complete and ready for its transcribing, it dawned on me I had not written its conclusion, as I had no conscious idea at the time as to how it was going to come about and most definitely when it would occur. Still, I knew deep within myself that I, in fact, had the conclusion of this book, yet it had not been physically birthed.

As I stepped away from these sometimes poignant thoughts and went about my normal daily endeavors, one of which included my speaking to my brother "Toney," who resided in Michigan, by way of telephone at that time. He had suggested to me on more than one occasion, even before my physical commencement of writing this book, to consider audibly recording my random thoughts. As he had noticed on numerous impromptu occasions, I appeared more fluently able to relate these beautiful laws without my awareness of it. Sometime after our conversation, one morning after my morning meditation ritual, I, in fact, decided, somewhat reluctantly, to do just that, to record my personal thoughts as I was having them.

As I sat on the veranda at my home that March morning of 2009 and loaded the cassette, I simply labeled it "Jacqueline's thoughts," as indeed I felt that they were just my own personal thoughts, being similar to what one would write in their own personal diary, never intending it to be heard, or in this case read. Yet after my listening to what I had recorded, I was indeed astonished to hear what I had actually recorded was as though the words were not of me, much less from me, yet they were, indeed, for me.

After I found myself listening to these recorded words, it seemed as though someone else was speaking to me and the words being conveyed to me filled my heart with a myriad of emotions all flowing abundantly and freely. Yes, those deep, poignant feelings of love, happiness, laughter, and tears totally engulfed me and gave me a highness I had never encountered before. I had never postulated these random thoughts would ever be appropriate to share in print for the public to read, yet after my listening to this audio tape numerous times, I was indeed enlightened that it was, in fact, intended for the conclusion of this book.

With these forethoughts, I present to you the conclusion of: "DREAM-IT-FIRST THE 80/20 LAW TO MANIFESTATION OF YOUR DREAM AND GOALS," as it was given and enlightened to me, apparently given and enlightened to me for you, by your greatest key.

SO, DREAMERS, LET'S GET STARTED!

THE CONCLUSION

Indeed you are made in the same image and likeness of God, the cosmic and great creator of all worthy dreams and goals, dreams available to each and every one who effortlessly seeks their full illumination, as has been shown and defined to you in this book you have just completed. God, regardless of the name you personally choose to use, is indeed a "Wonderful God!" "He's" surely everything good and awaits our full expression of Him through the enlightened dreams He has given to each and every one of us for our life here on this earth. This equates to all the beautiful and wanted qualities of love, joy, peace, happiness, prosperity, and abundance we all want and desire in our lives. Since you were created by God in His same likeness and image, we too possess those same beautiful and effortless qualities he possesses, yet this is not always consciously apparent to us as we strive in life for what was initially intended for us as "perfection" in our lives. So with this knowledge, if you are experiencing anything in your life right now, or in the past, anything "less than" this or that which deviates from God's same "likeness" and intentions for us that consists of those key effortless qualities of love, joy, peace, happiness, prosperity, and abundance in your life, then you must agree and know God's presence (your key 20 percent) mostly likely isn't or hasn't been there. How can it be, if you're not experiencing God's likeness in your life of love, joy, peace, happiness, prosperity, and abundance in your life? How does anyone experience God's presence and likeness? By simply incorporating and maintaining God's same consciousness. Yes! By simply keeping those same like qualities of God in the forefront of your mind at all times. This is with out fail the only cosmic 20 percent effort you need to ever apply in your life.

You have discovered in this book it is your inborn and innate right to have God's like qualities and full expression in your life of health, prosperity, and abundance in every single area of your life, individually expressed by you. You have seen God has this following blessing for you, "to make thee rich, and add no sorrow with it," as quoted in the Bible. Yet, when you are in full control of everything in your life, by your own choice, we are undoubtedly 80 percent or more of the time indeed not experiencing God's qualities, but those of sorrow and "lack," which is not from God, for He truly adds no sorrow, no lack, or limitation for your abundance in life. How can you be experiencing those things God has intended for you if you're in full control of everything? You may have bits and pieces of God's qualities, yet when you're in full 100 percent control of everything in your life, "in control of that family, in control of that job, in control of that business, in control of all the people in your lives," how can you possibly have this full control and be experiencing total love, joy, peace, prosperity, and abundance at the same time? Sounds kind of ludicrous, doesn't it?

It's impossible for you to be in full control of anything, experiencing and having an experience of God's qualities and presence at the same time. That's the reason why God instructs you to "Let go and let him." Let Him be the little 20 percent that will without fail take you to your 80 percent or greater good in your life, without fail, each and every time. It's only through God and your mind, which He has endowed you with, that you can have your heart's desire of love, joy, peace, prosperity, and abundance in your life. The only way you can "let go," that is, to totally let go (of any negative key 20 percents in your life), is by your "faith and belief," not so much into those dreams first, but in God first mentally, spiritually and emotionally first.

When you have this full faith and belief, you indeed may appear to those on the outside that you're "in full 100 percent control," yet it's your 100 percent faith and beautiful belief in God, controlling and providing you with beautiful love, happiness, joy, prosperity, and abundance in your life others view from afar. Yes, it may actually appear to others you are in full "control" of your life and are part of special 20 percent group in the world, effortlessly manifesting all your dreams in life, but you're not in control. God's in control and has always been there pioneering your 80 percent dreams in life on your behalf in His invisible and mysterious way. The only thing you've done is to just say what it is you want, that enlightened dream, and thereafter build a faith and a belief in that dream in your conscious mind, and then God does the mysterious and invisible controlling, for the manifestations of your dreams thereafter, through your 20 percent, which is your mind, as has been seen with the many people in this book you're just completed. When God, the greater 20 percent of all, is doing the controlling, you're not consumed in what would ordinarily be the burdens and sorrow of being in control, because you've in essence "letting go and letting God." You're then freer to do only your job of staying mentally, emotionally, and spiritually in congruency with your other 20 percent endowed to you: your enlightened dream. Your job is to "just be happy, prosperous, and healthy" in all areas expressed individually by you. That is indeed God's blessing for your life. That's maybe why the popular song you may have heard played many times in the '60s, and again in the '90s on your radio, has the lyrics "Don't Worry, Be Happy." Yes, we have indeed been instructed to "just be happy," not worrying and only building your faith and belief in that enlightened dream, not knowing or even caring about how and when that enlightened dream will occur. This is what gives you God's presence, and all His qualities of that peace, and that joy, that prosperity, and great abundance in your life. You see, it doesn't matter what roads you take in life; they always lead back to God.

I know that when you're in that beautiful state of being of, love, joy, peace, prosperity, and abundance, your mind is really being that of the same mind as God; that is, a mind of only "right consciousness" and "right thinking." The definition of "consciousness" is the "awareness of right and wrong."

You're in God's consciousness and that's the only consciousness of "right thinking." Everything's good! So you must always go back to that way of thinking. You must stay there. There's no kind of way you won't be consumed by the world if you don't have this "right thinking," if you don't have God's consciousness and presence in your life. It's a wonderful thing to know the qualities of God, because when you know God, you know yourself and those same qualities in yourself awaiting full expression out in the world, conveyed and express through your dreams in your life.

If you do not want to seek God first, then seek yourself first. When you seek yourself, in actuality, you're seeking God, because your mind is God's mind. So when you're seeking the good things in life, the love, the joy, the peace, prosperity, abundance, those things that are good in life, you are in actuality seeking God, "The Kingdom," for you and God are that beautiful "Kingdom."

In order to get to God, you have to go through yourself. When you go through God, you get to yourself. It doesn't really matter where you start, you just "seek first the kingdom," and then everything else (for God's good) will be added to you. It's such a beautiful revelation to understand these laws. Not to say that this is not always easy, because you do have your senses you perceive this outer world through. You have your vision, your hearing, your taste, and your smell, your touch all which you personally use to interpret this physical world. If you were to stay in this 80 percent physical world and not be on the 20 percent spiritual plane of knowing there's no truth behind those facts we perceive through those five sensory organs from the physical world, you will easily be caught up and consumed in this world, which only represents "lack and limitation." You know with God there's no such thing as "lack or limitation."

Your mind is the same mind as God! Only when you have and apply the conscious awareness of this knowledge, and these laws presented in this book, are you being an individual expression of God in this world! This is the awesome expression to express to the world. You can only be an individual awesome expression of God by keeping your thoughts and your thereafter actions in life integrated and in synergy with God's mind, which can be a challenge, a day-to-day challenge to be able to go back and connect, via spirit, and not be caught up in the appearances of things, (the 80 percent) the ostensible physical truths in things, the false "facts" that really hurt and take away your peace, your love, your happiness, your joy, your prosperity, and your abundance. These things are not from, or of, God.

Only with God are you able to go back to yourself, that person he originally created, full of love, joy, peace, happiness, prosperity, and abundance. You see, you can't do this world alone. You may try to do it alone over time. You may think you're doing it alone. Others may think you're doing it alone, but there's a void because you can't do this world over time without God. That's why I have repetitively said in this book aside from your basic 20 percent needs in life, food, water, shelter, clothing, air, oxygen, those basic needs, every other "real" need you now have or will ever have over time in this life will be a spiritual need, totally provided only by God.

I guess it has me in full astonishment as to why there's not more awareness of these laws presented in this book, and why this information is not more prevalent throughout the world today. This has been my major motivation for writing this book in such a fashion all people in all walks of life could easily understand regardless of their education, social status, race, religion, creed, faith, or other frames of reference. We indeed live in a highly intelligent society, yet it seems only approximately 20 percent or even less of the people even know these key spiritual truths I have presented in this little book, or are applying these truths in their lives. So with this said, would you say it's the 20 percent's responsibility to share with the 80 percent masses? I would definitely say yes to this question, for when "much is given" "much is expected."

In this book, "Dream It First: the 80/20 Law to Manifestation of Your Dreams and Goals," you have been able to discern the splendor of the beautiful laws that exist in the creation of all working dreams and goals in your life. It is a beautiful thing to have your key and higher power, who is the great creator of all creations enlighten to you, through your dreams and goals, your true intended dreams and missions in life, thereafter effortlessly over time in your life pioneering those beautiful enlightened dreams and goals into a manifestation for you.

It has indeed given me great pleasure, as well as great joy over this (key) time in my life, to have been able to share with you the key spirituals laws to manifesting all your dreams.

GOOD LUCK, DREAMERS !